Working With Aggressive Youth

A Sourcebook For Child-Care Providers

D1227690

Also from the Boys Town Press

Books

The Well-Managed Classroom
Teaching Social Skills to Youth
Effective Skills for Child-Care Workers
The Ongoing Journey: Awakening Spiritual Life in At-Risk Youth
Caring for Youth in Shelters
Helping Teens Unmask Sexual Con Games
Building Skills in High-Risk Families: Strategies for the Home-Based Practitioner
Common Sense Parenting
The SAY Books: Group Therapy for Sexually Abused Youth
I Think of My Homelessness
Letters from the Front
Boys Town: A Photographic History

Videos

Helping Your Child Succeed
Teaching Responsible Behavior
Videos for Parents Series
Sign With Me: A Family Sign Language Curriculum
Read With Me: Sharing the Joy of Storytelling with Your Deaf Toddler

For a free Boys Town Press catalog, call 1-800-282-6657.

Working With Aggressive Youth

A Sourcebook For Child-Care Providers

BOYS TOWN, NEBRASKA

Working With Aggressive Youth: A Sourcebook For Child-Care Providers

Published by The Boys Town Press
Father Flanagan's Boys' Home
Boys Town, Nebraska 68010

Publisher's Cataloging in Publication

(Prepared by Quality Books Inc.)

Working with aggressive youth: a sourcebook for child-care providers.

    p.cm.
    Originally published: Working with aggressive youth in open settings, 1989.
    Includes bibliographical references.
    ISBN 0-938510-16-9

    1. Social work with youth – United States. 2. Aggressiveness (Psychology) in youth – United States. 3. Child care – United States. I. Father Flanagan's Boys' Home.

HV1431.W67 1995   155.4'1247
                         QBI95 – 20592

Table of Contents

Introduction

Over the past 10 to 15 years, nationwide polls and crime statistics indicate an increased involvement of children under age 18 in violent crimes such as murder and assault.

Why are some of this nation's youth becoming more violent and antisocial? What are the root causes of these problems and what can be done to combat this rise in aggressive and antisocial behavior among teenagers?

As the American public becomes more aware of the growing problems of youth violence, questions regarding the causes and solutions to aggressive and antisocial youth behavior will be increasingly directed toward those individuals in our society who have been given the responsibility for dealing with these problems: probasion officers, school counselors, parent trainers, social workers, psychologists, child-care staff, foster parents, child-care administrators, and other professionals who work with aggressive children in both open and closed treatment settings.

In order to provide an effective response to these questions, human service professionals will need up-to-date information regarding the causes and potential solutions to aggressive youth behavior.

The first step in this process is training. This manual, and the skill-based training workshop which accompanies it, is designed to provide basic information to child-care staff who work with aggressive youth in open settings such as schools, clinics, group homes, foster homes, etc. Child-care staff who work with youth in closed settings (e.g. detention or locked psychiatric facilities) also will find the principles and procedures offered in this training useful in reducing the frequency and intensity of aggressive behavior in their programs. The teatment techniques presented in this training are nonphysical and nonaversive. They are derived from a comprehensive system of youth treatment technologies known as the Boys Town Family Home Program developed at Father Flanagan's Boys' Home near Omaha, Nebraska.

Boys Town

Popularly known as Boys Town, Father Flanagan's Boys' Home was founded in 1917 by Father Edward J. Flanagan. Currently, under the leadership of Father Val Peter, the Boys Town Family Home Program has four service programs: the Home Campus

Program that provides care for more than 500 boys and girls in 76 family-style group homes on a 1,500-acre campus at the site of the original Father Flanagan's Boys' Home in Boys Town, Nebraska; the Boys Town USA Program, whose goal is the development of wholly owned and operated Boys Town Family Homes around the country; the Boys Town Family Based Program, which provides crisis intervention, parent training, shelter care, and specialized foster care; and the Boys Town National Resource and Training Center, which provides training and technical assistance to other child-care organizations across the country.

The Boys Town Family Home Program

The Boys Town Family Home Program is a philosophy and a method of child care. The treatment program is based on the assumption that the youth whom it serves have not yet learned the necessary skills to live happy, healthy, and productive lives. The treatment approach focuses on the teaching of essential life skills to the youth in "family style" treatment setting (Peter, 1986). Social, academic, self-care, and vocational skills, as well as spiritual values, are taught in an active style with repeated practice, rehearsal, and reinforcement. A social skills curriculum composed of many prosocial behaviors is taught to the youth so they know which behaviors are most functional for them. They also know the situation in which these behaviors will produce the most beneficial outcomes.

This manual and the accompanying workshop training will focus on understanding aggressive behavior, teaching alternatives to aggressive behavior, and short-and lone-term strategies for defusing aggressive behaviors in youth.

The emphasis of this training will be on understanding and effectively dealing with the day-to-day occurrences of low-intensity, aggressive behavior such as noncompliance, teasing, whining, and scolding before they escalate into high-intensity aggressive behaviors like hitting, stabbing, and shooting. Aggressive behaviors emerge in mild forms and then evolve in intensity and form (Patterson, 1982). A developmental sequence of antisocial behavior begins in early childhool with such things as arguing, bragging, and demanding attention; this progresses in middle childhood to cruelty, fighting, poor peer relations, etc., eventually evolving into such adolescent behaviors as assault, theft, arson, substance abuse, and running away (Patterson, 1982).

A key variable in determining the progression of aggressive behavior from its mild to more extreme forms is the way these behaviors are addressed by child-care staff who interact with aggressive youth. This training is designed to provide child-care staff with a set of techniques for short-circuiting the progression of aggressive behavior in youth while also teaching youth prosocial alternatives to aggressive behavior.

Child-care staff who work in open settings are more likely to care for youth whose aggressive behaviors have not yet progressed to the more extreme forms of acting out such as rape, murder, and serious assault.

Because this workshop has been designed to assist child-care staff who work with aggressive youth in open settings, it is hoped that the skills acquired through this training will help them to effectively treat aggressive behaviors before they become so extreme that placement in a closed setting becomes the only option for a youth.

Chapter One

Overview Of Aggressive Behavior: What Do The Experts Say?

In order to treat aggressive behavior, it is important for child-care staff to know basic information about characteristics, correlates, and associated risk factors of aggressive youth. It is also helpful to have some notions about which of the various treatment approaches currently available for treating aggressive behavior show the most promise. Finally, a guiding theory which describes the development and maintenance of aggressive behavior will also aid child-care staff in conceptualizing the problems of aggressive youth.

This chapter will present information about aggressive youth compiled from a number of reviews regarding the treatment of antisocial and aggressive behavior in youth.

Aggression and Normal Development

Antisocial behavior encompasses a variety of specific acts such as fighting, stealing, lying, tempter outbursts, and noncompliance. However, it is important to note that many of the behaviors that are usually labeled as aggressive emerge in some form over the course of normal development. Antisocial behaviors such as fighting, negativism, destructiveness, etc., occur relatively often at different times during the course of a youth's development.

In normal populations, there are clear gender differences between boys and girls in regard to the type and amount of antisocial behavior they exhibit in the normal course of development. For example, MacFarlane, Allen, and Honzik (1954) found higher rates of stealing, truancy, destructiveness, and lying among boys over the course of normal development. Rutter, Tizard, and Whitmore (1970) reported two to three times as many boys as girls were involved in stealing, truancy, fighting, destructiveness, and bullying. A study conducted by Werry and Quay (1971) found that for a sample of youth between the ages of five to eight years old there was a prevalence among boys for significantly higher forms of antisocial behavior (e.g. fighting, stealing, gang involvement, temper tantrums, etc.) than for girls. Neurotic symptoms such as shyness, hypersensitivity, physical complaints, etc., were more frequent for girls across this age group. Overall results from numerous studies indicate that the rates of aggressive behavior tend to be higher among boys as the behaviors emerge over the course of normal development (Kazdin, 1985).

1

However, the most significant and comforting feature of aggressive behaviors among normal youth is that aggressive behavior tends to decrease dramatically over the course of normal development (Kazdin, 1985). An illustration of this was provided in a study conducted by MacFarlane et al. (1954) which compared the number of children reported by their mothers as engaging in lying and destructiveness (Figure 1).

If aggressive behavior emerges in the normal course of child development, why is it that some youth who become labeled as antisocial persist in these behaviors, while their normative peers show a decline in these behaviors over the course of their development from youth to adult? One explanation for the continued occurrence of aggressive behavior beyond the point at which these behaviors begin to drop off for normal children can be found in the work of Patterson (1982). Patterson's work with aggressive youth and their families has led him to suggest that family interaction may serve as basic training for aggression. Youth are trained to be aggressive in dysfunctional families whereby the interaction style among dysfunctional families, itself, maintains antisocial behavior (Patterson, Dishion, & Bank, 1984). According to Patterson's coercion theory, the continuance of aggressive behavior beyond the ages during which it diminishes in normal populations is a function of an arrested socialization process brought about by ineffective family management practices (Patterson & Stouthamer-Loeber, 1984).

Correlates of Aggressive And Antisocial Behavior

Antisocial behaviors are likely to occur together and to form a syndrome or a constellation of symptoms (Kazdin, 1985; Patterson, 1982). Antisocial behavior as a syndrome can include several core symptoms such as fighting, truancy, theft, and temper tantrums. Destroying one's own or another person's property, defying, threatening others, and running away also may be seen as behaviors which are part of this syndrome. The presence of a particular symptom of aggression in youth diagnosed as antisocial, conduct disordered, etc., usually indicates that a number of other symptoms are likely to be present (Glueck & Glueck, 1950; Robins, 1966). Among alternative symptoms that have been found in antisocial youth, those related to hyperactivity have been most frequently identified (Kazdin, 1985). Antisocial youth suffer from academic deficiencies which are reflected in achievement level, grades, and specific skill areas, particularly reading (Ledingham & Schwartzman, 1984; Sturge, 1982). Poor peer relations also are likely to correlate to antisocial and aggressive behavior (Behar & Stewart, 1982; Lesser, 1959; Dishion, Loeber, Stouthamer-Loeber & Patterson, 1984).

Gender

As is the case with normal youth, analysis across many clinical settings indicates that boys are much more likely than girls to be referred to aggressiveness, stealing, lying, etc. (Ackerson, 1931; Gilbert, 1957; Robins, 1966). Apart from differences in the types of

FIGURE 1

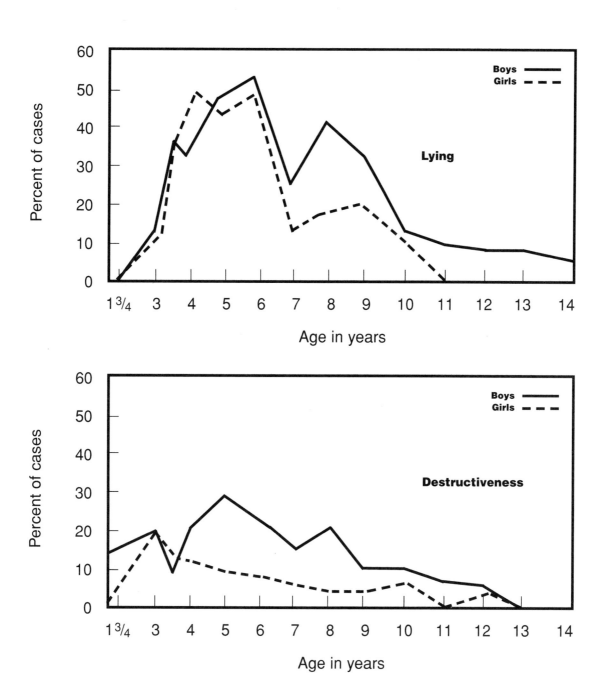

Source: Kazdin A. E. (1985). **Treatment of Antisocial Behavior in Children and Adolescents.** Homewood, IL: The Dorsey Press. Taken from: MacFarlane, J.W., Allen, L., & Honzik, M.P. (1954). **A developmental study of the behavior problems of normal children between 21 months and 14 years.** Berkeley and Los Angeles: University of California Press. Reprinted by permission of Brooks/Cole Publishing Company, Pacific Grove, CA 93950.

aggressive behavior displayed among boys and girls, research suggests that there are gender differences in the age of onset of dysfunction (Robins). Robins found that the onset of antisocial behavior for boys was concerned in the eight- to ten-year-old range. For girls, the onset of antisocial behavior was concentrated in the 14- to 16-year-old range. Robins also found that the type of symptom picture for antisocial boys and girls appears to be different. For boys, aggression was the most likely presenting problem, and for girls, the antisocial behavior was much more likely to include sexual behavior. In addition, specific referral symptoms for girls would include behavior such as cruelty, destructiveness, and sexual problems. In general, the data suggests clear differences in aggressive behavior as a function of gender.

Stability of Aggressive Behavior

The notion that youth will eventually outgrow aggressive behavior as they mature over time has been questioned by a number of researchers (Kazdin, 1985). Patterson (1982) has indicated that there is a remarkable stability and continuity of aggressive behavior over the course of development for youth referred to treatment for aggressive behavior. Adults who are sociopathic invariably have a history of antisocial behavior as youth. Paterson has suggested that there is an orderly sequence in the development of antisocial behavior from higher- to lower-rate symptoms. Deviance progresses from less to more extreme forms of behavior and there is a transition in the progression such that youth who exhibit the more extreme forms of behavior also will have performed the preceding behaviors in the sequence. Cross-sectional studies also suggest

a likely progression of symptoms among aggressive youth (Edelbrock, 1983). The developmental sequence of antisocial behaviors usually begins in early childhood with such behaviors as arguing, bragging, and demanding attention. In middle childhood, behaviors like cruelty, fighting, lying, cheating, poor peer relations, destructiveness, and stealing in the home begin to emerge. By the onset of adolescence, antisocial behaviors take new forms such as fire-setting, stealing outside of the home, running away, vandalism, and substance abuse. Antisocial behaviors emerge in mild forms and then evolve in intensity and form, going from overt and high frequency behaviors, such as fighting and teasing, to more covert and low frequency behaviors like setting fires and stealing outside of the home.

Major Risk Factors Associated With Aggressive and Antisocial Behavior

Parent and Family Factors

Specific antisocial and maladaptive parental behaviors clearly increase the risk of these same behaviors in youth (Kazdin, 1985). Criminal behavior and alcoholism, particularly in the father, have been two of the stronger and consistently demonstrated factors that increase the youth's risk for antisocial behavior (Robins, 1966; Rutter & Giller, 1983; West, 1982). In addition, Glueck and Glueck (1968) found that the grandparents of antisocial youth are more likely to show antisocial behavior compared to the grandparents of youth who are not antisocial. It appears that the risk for antisocial behavior may be associated with a line of succession in these behaviors which cuts across generations. In a sense, aggressive patterns of behavior are transmitted within the family and passed on to successive generations.

Parent and Youth Interaction

Antisocial youth are more likely than normal youth to be victims of child abuse and to be in homes where spouse abuse is evident (Behar & Stewart, 1982).

Parents of aggressive and antisocial youth tend to be harsh in their attitudes toward disciplinary practices (Farrington, 1978; Nye, 1958). However, the increased risk for antisocial behavior is not entirely due to harsher punishment. Studies have shown that more lax, erratic, and inconsistent discipline by one or both parents is related to aggression. Severe punishment on the part of the father and lax discipline on the part of the mother have been implicated in antisocial behavior (McCord, McCord, & Zola, 1959). Patterson (1982) also suggests that parents of aggressive youth are particularly unskilled in their use of punishment for these behaviors. Patterson also has found through direct observation of families in their natural homes that parents of aggressive youth are more likely to give commands to their youth, to reward aggressive behavior, and to ignore or provide aversive consequences for prosocial behavior. Finally, parents of aggressive youth are less likely to monitor the whereabouts of their youth or to make arrangements for their care when the parents are temporarily out of the home (Kazdin, 1985).

Broken Homes and Marital Discord

Separation of one's parents during childhood has been implicated in antisocial and delinquent behavior (Glueck & Glueck, 1968). Unhappy marital relationships, interperson conflicts, and aggression characterize the parental relationships of many aggressive children (Hetherington & Martin, 1979; Rutter & Giller, 1983). However, the major risk factor associated with broken homes and marital discord is the extent of the discord that exists between the father and mother. Thus, discord rather than separation and divorce is seen as a major risk factor (Kazdin, 1985).

Birth Order and Family Size

Birth order has been implicated in the onset of antisocial behavior. Evidence suggests that antisocial behaviors are greater among middle children in comparison to only, first-born, or youngest children (Nye, 1958; Wadsworth, 1979).

Social Class And Economic Disadvantage

There is a preponderance of antisocial behavior and delinquency among youth from lower socio-economic groups (West, 1982). However, the relationship is not strong within individual studies and not consistently evident across investigations (Robins, 1978).

School-Related Factors

A consistent finding has been that antisocial youth suffer from academic and school deficiencies (Farrington, 1978; Hirschi & Hindeland, 1977; Wolfgang, Figlio, & Sellin, 1972). It is clear that early academic problems constitute a risk factor for antisocial behavior (Dishion et al., 1984) suggest that academic skill deficits may be the strongest correlate of antisocial behavior.

The Prognosis for Aggressive and Antisocial Youth

The long-term prognosis for aggressive and antisocial youth is bleak when aggressive and antisocial behaviors go untreated.

Studies have shown that youth who are identified by the courts or referred through clinical agencies often have a poor prognosis for successful adjustment as adults (Glueck & Glueck, 1968). In a now-classic study by Robins (1966), antisocial behavior in youth predicted multiple problems in adulthood. Youth who have been referred to treatment for antisocial behavior suffer wide ranging dysfunctions as adults including psychiatric problems, criminal behavior, and physical and social adjustments. Figure 2 summarizes the types of problems aggressive and antisocial youth can experience in adulthood when problem behaviors in childhood go untreated.

But not all antisocial youth become antisocial adults. Major factors that cause antisocial youth to continue their behavior into adulthood are summarized in Figure 3.

Treatment for Aggressive And Antisocial Behavior: What Works?

Child-care staff who work with aggressive youth need to know which of the treatments currently available show the greatest promise for helping aggressive youth. In what follows, a number of popular treatment approaches will be reviewed in regard to their basic approach to treating aggressive behaviors. Evidence of the treatment efficacy of these different approaches also will be presented. This review is based on a more extensive review conducted by Kazdin (1985).

Psychotherapy (Individual and Group)

Psychotherapy is based on intrapsychic views of the nature of deviant behavior in youth. Intrapsychic processes are viewed as being responsible for maladjustment in youth. Therapy in primarily directed toward helping the youth bring into his or her awareness certain thoughts, feelings, and experiences that are then worked through with a therapist. A strong relationship with the therapist is important to assist the youth in the expression and resolution of important feelings, experiences, etc., which lead to therapeutic change.

Kazdin's (1985) review of the psychotherapeutic literature indicated that relatively few studies focused specifically on the treatment of antisocial youth and adolescents. In general, intrapsychic approaches are laden with untested theory both for the development of deviance and the delineation of key treatment variables.

Psychotherapeutic techniques tend to be relatively nonspecific, making it difficult to judge treatment effects or to replicate psychotherapeutic procedures. Consequently, the outcome evidence regarding psychotherapy is not strong enough to determine the efficacy of psychotherapeutic treatment modalities. Although individual psychotherapists may experience clinical success in treatment aggressive youth, there is a little evidence that individual or group psychotherapy as a whole impacts antisocial behavior (Kazdin, 1985).

Family Therapy

Family therapy, in general, focuses its treatment efforts on the entire family as a group, rather than on a given individual in the family such as an aggressive youth. Family therapy is centered on the examination of

FIGURE 2
LONG-TERM PROGNOSIS OF YOUTH IDENTIFIED AS ANTISOCIAL

Antisocial youth as adults are more likely to show ...

Area of functioning	Characteristics in adulthood
1. Psychiatric status	Greater psychiatric impairment including sociopathic personality, alcohol and drug abuse, and isolated symptoms (e.g. anxiety, somatic complaints); also, greater history of psychiatric hospitalization.
2. Criminal behavior	Higher rates of criminal behavior, arrest records and conviction, and period of time spent in jail.
3. Occupational adjustment	Higher unemployment, shorter history of employment, lower-status jobs, more frequent change of jobs, earning lower wages, and depending more frequently on financial assistance (welfare). Served less frequently and performed less well in the armed services.
4. Educational attainment	Higher rate of dropping out of school, lower attainment among those who remain in school.
5. Marital status	Higher rates of divorce, remarriage, and separation.
6. Social participation	Less contact with relatives, friends, and neighbors; little participation in organizations such as church.
7. Physical health	Higher mortality rate; higher rate of hospitalization of physical (as well as psychiatric) problems.

Source: Kazdin A. E. (1985). **Treatment of Antisocial Behavior in Children and Adolescents.** Homewood, IL: The Dorsey Press. Reprinted by permission of Brook/Cole Publishing Company, Pacific Grove, CA 93950.

FIGURE 3
FACTORS THAT PREDICT ANTISOCIAL BEHAVIOR IN ADULTHOOD

Youths are more likely to continue their antisocial behavior as adults to the extent that they show . . .

Characteristic	Specific Pattern
1. **Age of onset**	Earlier onset (e.g. before 10 or 12) of their antisocial behavior. Early onset also is related to rate and seriousness of later antisocial behavior.
2. **Breadth of deviance**	A greater number of different types of antisocial behaviors; a greater variety of situations in which antisocial behavior is manifest (e.g. at home, school); a greater range of persons or organizations against which such behaviors are expressed.
3. **Frequency of antisocial behavior**	A greater number of different antisocial episodes independent of whether they include a number of different behaviors.
4. **Seriousness of the behavior**	Relatively serious antisocial behavior in childhood, especially if the behavior could be grounds for adjudication.
5. **Types of symptoms**	The following specific antisocial behaviors: lying, impulsiveness, truancy, running away, theft, and staying out late. Also, nonantisocial symptoms of slovenliness and enuresis after age six.
6. **Parent characteristics**	Parent psychopathology, particularly if antisocial behavior; father has record of arrest, unemployment, alcoholism; poor parental supervision of child; overly strict, lax, or inconsistent discipline.
7. **Family**	Greater if from homes with marital discord and larger family.

Source: Kazdin A. E. (1985). **Treatment of Antisocial Behavior in Children and Adolescents.** Homewood, IL: The Dorsey Press. Reprinted by permission of Brooks/Cole Publishing Company, Pacific Grove, CA 93950.

communication and interaction patterns between family members. Treatment may vary along a number of dimensions (e.g. co-therapists, concurrent individual therapy, etc.), and therapists can assume several different roles as the treatment process unfolds. In general, the problem behavior of a given individual in the family is seen as reflecting a problem in the family system as a whole and interpersonal relationships between members. Changes in the way the entire family functions together as a unit are thought to produce changes in individual family members.

Like psychotherapy, there is little research regarding the effectiveness of family therapy for treating aggressive and antisocial youth (Kazdin, 1985). Although family crisis intervention has demonstrated an ability to prevent psychiatric hospitalization, many family therapy modalities do not focus on the outcome behavior of the youth who displays aggressive behaviors. In addition, family therapy treatment procedures are rarely specified well enough so that empirical studies or replications of treatment are possible.

Functional Family Therapy (Klein, Alexander, & Parsons, 1977) has demonstrated more success than psychotherapeutic or client-centered family therapies in reducing delinquency in target youth and preventing sibling referrals to treatment. With the exception of Functional Family Therapy, the general empirical evidence regarding family therapy provides minimal support for the use of family therapy as a viable treatment for antisocial youth (Kazdin, 1985).

Behavior Therapy

Behavior therapy is predicated on the idea that aggressive and antisocial behaviors are learned responses which result from the interaction between the youth and other key persons (e.g. parents, siblings, and peers) who comprise the youth's social environment.

Learning principles and procedures such as reinforcement and punishment play a key role in the treatment of aggressive behavior. Treatment focuses on manipulating antecedent and consequent variables which affect behavior in an attempt to decrease dysfunctional behaviors while developing and strengthening prosocial responses. Behavior therapy encompasses a large number of well-specified and easily replicated techniques for producing behavior change.

Numerous studies have demonstrated the efficacy of behavioral treatment techniques in altering aggressive behavior (Kazdin, 1985). The overall evidence suggests that aggressive behaviors can be suppressed, but long-term treatment effects often are not demonstrated. Behavior therapy shows promise in reducing aggressive behavior, but much more attention needs to be given to the generalization of treatment effects over time.

Parent Management Training

Parent Management Training (PMT) includes several procedures which are designed to train parents to interact with their children in beneficial ways. Training is based on the perspective that aggressive youth behaviors are unwittingly developed and maintained by dysfunctional family management practices. The focus of training is directed to the ongoing parent-child interactions that occur daily. PMT is designed to change the pattern of child-parent interaction so that prosocial rather than aggressive behavior is strengthened and supported in the family.

Initially, training is directed toward the goal of developing specific parenting skills. After parenting skills are developed, the program focuses on helping parents to effectively address the problematic behaviors of their children (Kazdin, 1987).

PMT procedures, especially those developed by Patterson (1982) and his colleagues, have shown both short- and long-term treatment effects in working with aggressive youth. When compared to other modalities, PMT shows better results at two- and five-year post-treatment intervals (Kazdin, 1987). Studies also indicate that this treatment approach makes many demands on the parents who participate in their training. For parents who themselves suffer from severe forms of dysfunctional behavior (e.g. depression, alcoholism, etc.), the demands of this training may be too great for them to successfully carry it out.

Overall, PMT has been described as one of the most promising treatment modalities for treating aggressive and antisocial youth (Kazdin, 1987).

Cognitive Problem-Solving Skills Training

Problem-Solving Skills Training (PSST) focuses on changing the aggressive youth's thought processes or cognitions (e.g. self-statements, perceptions, attributions, etc.) that are thought to play a role in the youth's aggressive behavior (Kazdin, 1987). There are numerous forms of PSST, but in general they share certain treatment characteristics.

Common characteristics of PSST approaches include an emphasis on altering the thought processes youth employ when approaching certain interpersonal situations, step-by-step approaches to problem-solving, use of structured tasks such as games and stories, and the active involvement of the therapist in treatment (Kazdin, 1987).

Outcome studies regarding PSST have shown that this form of training can alter cognitive styles, but does not substantially impact targeted aggressive behavior. Better outcomes of treatment result when PSST is combined with direct consequences for aggressive behaviors. In general, PSST does produce change in youth with mild adjustment problems (Kazdin, 1985). PSST shows some promise as a treatment for aggressive youth because of its specificity, particularly when it is applied to real-life situations, and paired with effective consequences. PSST deserves closer exploration as a treatment technique for aggressive behavior, but as yet it has not been shown to be an effective treatment for antisocial behavior.

Pharmacotherapy

Pharmacotherapy is based on evidence which suggests that, for some youth, there may be a biological basis to their aggressive behavior. Pharmacotherapy involves the use of various drugs (e.g. stimulants, antidepressants, antimanics, etc.) to control aggression in children and youth.

To date, there is no established drug treatment which can be broadly applied to treating aggressive behavior in youth. This is due, in part, to the fact that aggression is correlated with a wide range of other nonbiological attributes (e.g. family history, sex, age, etc.).

However, certain classes of drugs such as stimulants and antidepressants have been effective with some aggressive youth. For example, lithium, an antimanic drug, has shown some promise as a treatment for impulsive-aggressive disorders in youth between the ages of 16 and 23 (Sheard, 1975). Studies also suggest that antisocial behaviors which accompany hyperactivity may be altered with stimulant medication (Kazdin, 1985).

The use of pharmacotherapy as a treatment for aggressive behavior is worth exploring for some specific classes of aggressive youth. However, the use of pharmacotherapy as a treatment for aggressive youth should be supplemented with nondrug therapies. In addition, due to the damaging short- and long-term side effects of certain drugs, pharmacotherapy as a treatment for youth should be undertaken with much caution.

Designing Interventions For Aggressive Youth

A review of the available approaches for treating aggressive youth indicates that there is some empirical evidence to support the efficacy of certain treatment modalities. Primary contenders would include parent management training, behavioral family therapy, behavior therapy, cognitive problem-solving skills training, and certain forms of pharmacotherapy (Kazdin, 1985). However, any one of these treatment approaches does not address all of the treatment needs of aggressive youth. Each treatment modality has certain strengths and limitations. When designing treatment interventions for aggressive youth, it has been suggested that broad-based approaches which incorporate the best features of a number of specific treatment modalities be developed into a comprehensive package of treatment interventions (Kazdin, 1985); for example, the integration of techniques from Parent Management Training,

and behavior therapy. The combination of these treatment modalities into a broad-based treatment approach would seem reasonable because of the evidence of their individual effects and the compatibility of their integration (Kazdin, 1985).

A Developmental Model Of Antisocial Behavior

During the last 20 years, Gerald Patterson and his colleagues at the Oregon Social Learning Center have been researching a developmental model of aggressive and antisocial behavior (Patterson, DeBaryshe, & Ramsey, 1989). According to this model, chronic delinquency may result from a progression of developmental experiences beginning in early childhood which are affected by family management practices and characteristics.

Family Management Practices

Patterson's developmental model of aggressive behavior is predicated on the notion that disruptions in family management practices and irritable exchanges between the aggressive youth and other family members provides the basic training ground for the development, evolution, and maintenance of aggressive behavior from early childhood through adolescence (Patterson et al., 1984). This view of aggressive behavior is based on a social learning theory perspective which asserts that aggressive behaviors are learned responses that are acquired through inadvertent training in dysfunctional families. The youth's behavior problems are unwittingly developed and maintained by inappropriate parent-child interactions. Aggression or other deviant behaviors performed by a youth and directed toward a parent – usually the mother – and other siblings, are strengthened when the parent gives in or complies. The parent obtains the short-term relief of ending a power struggle, but in the process rewards the youth's aggressive behavior, ensuring future occurrences.

Patterson (1982) has labeled the process whereby family members learn to control each other through aggressive acts as coercion. Coercion characterizes a social-interactional style exhibited by dysfunctional families. The term coercion means using unpleasant behaviors to get what you want. One reason coercion is used in families is that it is an effective way to get things accomplished.

Coercion begins when one member of a family introduces an unpleasant event into ongoing family behavior. For example, a parent may ask a youth to put away his or her toys. The youth perceives the parent's request as an unpleasant event and responds by engaging in some behavior that is annoying to the parent. The youth's behavior is most often noncompliant in form (e.g. whining, crying, talking back, ignoring, etc.). The parent then attempts to scold the youth for noncompliance, but the youth intensifies the noncompliant behavior. Both parent and youth continue to exchange unpleasant events until one or the other gives in. If the parent gives in, which is often the case, the youth's aggressive responses are strengthened. The parent also is likely to give in more often in similar encounters in the future due to an inability to teach his or her children to follow requests or directions.

In dysfunctional families, these brief encounters can occur hundreds of times a day. Over time, these encounters intensify, and disruptive episodes between family members get longer and longer. Both parent and child end up inflicting greater amounts of pain on each other. The best way to win an argument in a coercive process is to dramatically intensify the pain to the other person by doing or saying something that really hurts him or her. This has a powerful effect on the other person, who almost always withdraws, ending the showdown. Aggressive youth exhibit a fairly predictable progression of coercive behaviors which they escalate over time. For example, in response to requests, a youth may first learn that ignoring his or her parents is successful in avoiding them. Gradually the youth learns that a temper tantrum is even more effective in avoiding requests.

These aggressive behaviors often generalize to other situations as a learned way of getting what one wants. For example, the aggressive youth begins to fight with other youth (e.g. siblings, peers, etc.) in order to control them. As Patterson and Forgatch (1987) have noted, the long-term consequences for using unpleasant events, or the threat of them to control other family members, are disastrous. The outcome of the coercive family process is that the parents unknowingly train their children to perform antisocial behaviors.

Once a youth has developed a strong repertoire of coercive and antisocial behaviors, the youth's parents often begin to reject the youth and interact with him or her less often, precluding opportunities for social reinforcement of appropriate behaviors. Consequently, the youth does not acquire important social skills for getting along with others which are prerequisites for success in school and later employment (Figure 4).

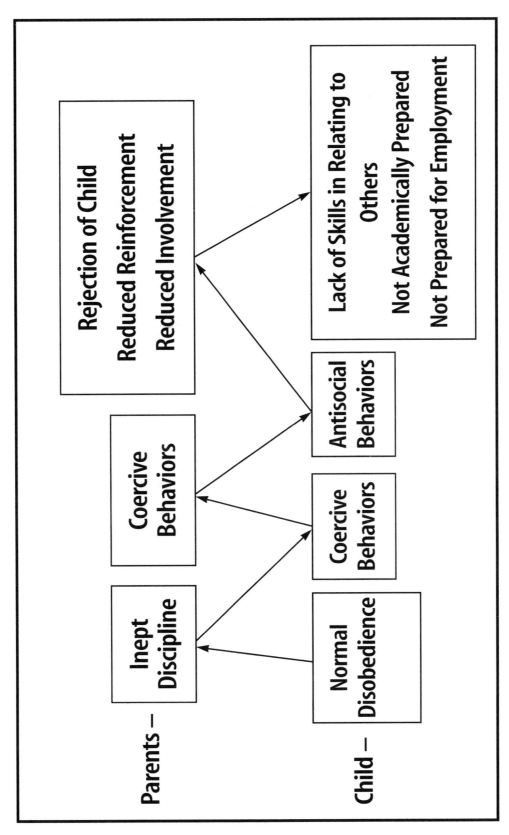

FIGURE 4 COERCIVE FAMILY PROCESS

Source: Forgatch, M.S. (1985). **A Social Learning Approach to Family Therapy.** Workshop presented at the Taboroff Child and Adolescent Psychiatry Conference on Conduct Disorders in Children and Adolescents. Snowbird, UT; February 24–27.

All youth engage in coercive behavior to some degree, especially during early childhood, and certain levels of coercion are present in all families. However, not all families end up training their children to become aggressive and antisocial. Why are some families more successful than others in breaking the coercive process and teaching their children more prosocial methods of getting their needs met? It appears that the acquisition of key family management practices is an important variable in helping youth to make the transition from coercive to normative behavior (Patterson & Stouthamer-Loeber, 1984).

Four sets of family management skills that appear to play a key role in normative youth development have been identified by Patterson (1982). They are: monitoring a youth's whereabouts, the use of effective discipline for coercive and aggressive behavior, family problem-solving skills, and the development and encouragement of prosocial youth behavior. Dysfunctional families have been shown to be deficient in a number of these key family management practices (Patterson & Stouthamer-Loeber, 1984).

Factors Which Disrupt Family Management Practices

Why is it that certain families engage in highly maladaptive family practices when others do not? It appears that a number of key factors play an important role in the disruption of effective family management practices (Patterson et al., 1989).

Family History

As mentioned earlier, a history of antisocial behavior by a youth's parents and grandparents puts him or her at risk for developing antisocial behaviors. Patterson et al. (1989) assert that antisocial parents are very likely to exhibit ineffective discipline practices.

Family Demographics

The parents' race, education level, occupation, neighborhood, and income can all relate to the incidence of severe antisocial behavior in youth (Patterson et al., 1989). For example, Patterson, Reid, and Dishion (1989) found that uneducated parents with unskilled jobs were significantly ineffective in disciplining, monitoring, problem-solving, and reinforcement for their children. These types of parenting skills were mentioned earlier as critical for supporting normal youth development.

Family Stressors

Families that are stressed by disruptive factors such as marital conflict, financial problems, substance abuse, etc., also are less likely to acquire or exhibit effective family management practices (Patterson et al., 1989).

In summary, families that must contend with a number of these disruptive variables (e.g. history of antisocial behavior, disadvantages socioeconomic status, marital conflict, etc.) have a higher probability of exhibiting ineffective family management practices. Disrupted family management practices, in turn, provide fertile ground for the development of coercive family processes which produce antisocial behavior in youth (Figure 5).

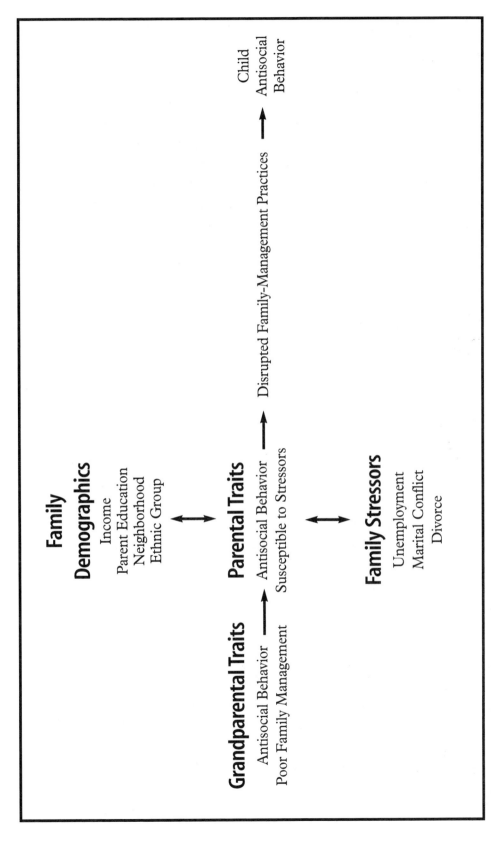

FIGURE 5 DISRUPTORS OF EFFECTIVE PARENTING

Family Demographics
Income
Parent Education
Neighborhood
Ethnic Group

Grandparental Traits
Antisocial Behavior
Poor Family Management

Parental Traits
Antisocial Behavior
Susceptible to Stressors

Family Stressors
Unemployment
Marital Conflict
Divorce

Disrupted Family-Management Practices

Child Antisocial Behavior

Source: Patterson, G. R., DeBaryshe, B. D., and Ramsey, E. (1989). A Developmental Perspective on Antisocial Behavior. **The American Psychologist**, 44(2), 329-335.

Development Progression Of Antisocial Behavior

Once the stage for coercive processes in the family has been set in early childhood, a second stage occurs. Youth who have acquired coercive behaviors but are deficient in prosocial skills begin to experience a new set of problems in middle childhood. The two most serious are academic failure and peer refection (Dishion et al., 1984). Because dysfunctional families are unable to break the cycle of coercive behaviors in early childhood, these behaviors continue and intensify.

When these youth enter school they come into conflict with teachers and peers due to their coercive behaviors and general lack of social skills. These youth experience difficulty getting along with others, forming intimate relationships, negotiating compromises, completing homework, etc. The coercive youth in middle childhood may be labeled by agents external to the family as abrasive, obnoxious, extremely shy, etc., while lacking the interpersonal problem-solving skills that would enable them to resist tempting situations, work out conflicts with peers, and avoid problems with others (Dishion et al., 1984). Academic failure and a general lack of social skills often results in rejection by normal peers leading the coercive youth to gravitate toward a group of similarly unskilled youth.

Academic failure and peer rejection set the occasion for the final developmental stage of a conduct disorder: identification with a deviant peer group. Antisocial behavior and peer group rejection are important prerequisites to membership in a deviant peer group (Snyder, Dishion, & Patterson, 1986). Association with an antisocial peer group in early adolescence provides the coercive youth with ample opportunities to acquire specific attitudes, motivations, and rationalizations to support antisocial behavior and the performance of delinquent acts (Patterson et al., 1989).

In summary, disrupted family management practices in early and middle childhood contribute to an arrested socialization process. The outcomes of this arrested socialization process are identification with other antisocial youth and commitment to a deviant lifestyle (Figure 6).

As stated earlier in this chapter, the long-term prognosis for conduct-disordered youth who continue along this developmental path is poor. As adults, these youth are more likely to experience a number of negative live outcomes including employment problems, marital difficulties, substance abuse, incarceration, and institutionalization (Patterson et al., 1989).

Treating the Aggressive Youth

It appears that serious antisocial acts such as robbery, rape, and assault are rooted in early childhood experiences within the family. Patterson's (1982) developmental perspective of antisocial behavior informs us that parental child-rearing practices in early childhood play a major role in determining both prosocial and deviant youth behaviors. It is entirely possible that the problems of a 16-year-old charged with aggravated assault began when he was a young child because his parents were unable to teach him simple compliance behaviors, such as following instructions, accepting "No" answers, and accepting criticism. The work of Patterson and others strongly suggests that family management practices have been found to correlate consis-

FIGURE 6 A DEVELOPMENTAL PROGRESSION FOR ANTISOCIAL BEHAVIOR

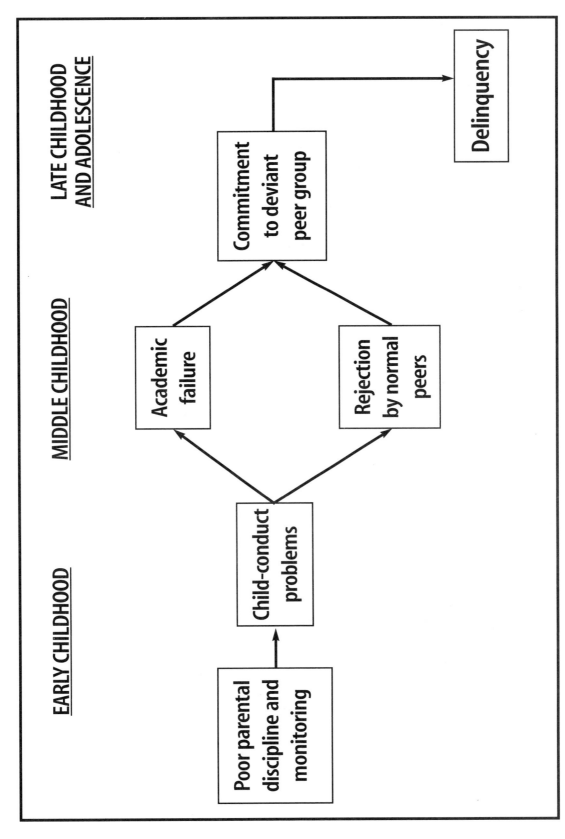

| EARLY CHILDHOOD | MIDDLE CHILDHOOD | LATE CHILDHOOD AND ADOLESCENCE |

Poor parental discipline and monitoring → Child-conduct problems

Child-conduct problems → Academic failure

Child-conduct problems → Rejection by normal peers

Academic failure → Commitment to deviant peer group

Rejection by normal peers → Commitment to deviant peer group

Commitment to deviant peer group → Delinquency

tently with antisocial behavior. As previously mentioned, specific family management practices that are deficient in the parents of aggressive youth include monitoring their child's whereabouts, use of effective discipline for aggressive behavior, employment of effective problem-solving skills for handling crisis situations, and perhaps most important, the teaching and support of prosocial behavior (Patterson & Forgatch, 1987). It follows then that teaching parents how to monitor, discipline, problem-solve, and reinforce their children's behaviors are elements of a treatment approach for working with aggressive youth.

A number of studies have empirically verified this approach as a viable treatment for aggressive behavior (Patterson, 1982).

However, many aggressive youth who reside in placements outside of their natural home may be beyond the scope of a family-based intervention. Such is the case with the majority of youth who reside at Boys Town.

The purpose of this manual and the skill-based workshop which accompanies it is to provide child-care staff who work with aggressive youth in open settings the same set of skills that might have aided these youth's natural parents. We believe these skills can be generalized to out-of-home settings because they have formed the basis for the treatment techniques of Boys Town's Family Home Program. Essentially, this training should teach child-care staff how to effectively monitor the behavior of aggressive youth, employ effective discipline in dealing with the aggressive acts, teach cognitive problem-solving skills to aggressive youth, and support the development of prosocial behaviors as alternatives to aggression for the youth in their care.

Chapter Two

Assessing Aggressive Behavior In Children

Many of the treatment techniques employed in the Boys Town Family Home Program have social learning theory and applied behavior analysis as their conceptual base. A behavioral approach to treatment emphasizes a functional analysis of the social environment to determine the causes of behavior, active approaches to behavior change, a focus of current performance, ongoing evaluation of change efforts, and program revision based on evaluation results.

A Behavior Approach To Treatment

Traditional models of child care often are based on a medical model of therapeutic treatment. According to this approach, children's problems result from internal psychopathology (e.g. mental illness). Typically, professionally trained therapists are entrusted with the responsibility of performing treatment. Consequently, staff who work directly with children and youth are asked to provide a "warm, safe, nurturing, and supportive" environment for the persons in their care. Supervisors such as caseworkers, psychologists, and psychiatrists are the ones who actually deliver treatment in the form of individual and group therapy.

Such therapy focuses on attempts to get children to understand themselves and to achieve insight regarding the reasons they behave in certain ways.

Behavioral treatment programs have a significantly different view of treatment. Problem behavior is viewed as a historical result of inadequate learning and motivation to perform socially acceptable behavior. Behavior problems are due to a lack of essential life skills which result from poor modeling, inadequate training, and weak or ineffective incentives for the learning of necessary skills. Treatment is based on an educational, rather than an illness, model.

The goal of behavioral treatment is to teach youth a range of social, academic, pre-vocational, self-care, and family-living skills. Teaching is comprised of a series of instructions, modeling, practice, and feedback sessions. Because of this orientation toward treatment, many of the problem behaviors exhibited by youth can be successfully remediated by direct-care staff.

The Causes of Behavior

From a behavioral point of view, aggressive behavior arises from the interaction of three primary causal sources: the biological effects of one's genetic makeup, the long-term environmental effects of one's social learning history, and the immediate environmental effects of conditions which prevail in one's current social environment.

Hereditary Factors And Aggressive Behavior

A number of empirical studies can be cited in support of the role of genetic factors as causal agents contributing to the emergence of aggressive behavior. Studies of twins have shown a great degree of concordance of antisocial behavior among identical twins (Christiansen, 1974; Cloninger, Reich, & Guze, 1978). Adoption studies have shown that antisocial behavior in children is greater when the biological parents had a history of antisocial behavior than when they did not (Cadoret, 1978; Crowe, 1974).

Many studies of antisocial behavior have focused on biochemical deficiencies. In one study, altered serotonin metabolism was associated with aggressive and suicidal behavior in a small sample of aggressive adults (Brown et al., 1982). Other researchers have identified higher levels of plasma testosterone among violent delinquents as compared to normal controls (Mattsson, Schalling, Olweus, Low & Svensson, 1980).

In addition, other biological factors have been evaluated as possible causal agents. Mednick (1978), for example, suggests that inherited arousal patterns of the autonomic nervous system may influence the extent to which antisocial person fail to learn to inhibit antisocial behavior.

There is ample evidence to support the notion that hereditary factors can play a causal role in the development of aggressive behaviors. However, as Kazdin (1985) points out, genetic factors neither account solely for the emergence of aggressive behaviors nor are they present in all individuals who display aggression. Of equal importance are the effects of an individual's social environment. For example, the combined contribution of genetic and environmental factors can be seen in studies which have shown that the occurrence of antisocial behavior, in both biological and adoptive parents, increases the risk of antisocial behavior in children (Mednick & Hutchings, 1978). The work of Patterson (1982) also clearly illustrates the role of non-biological factors, such as family management practices, that contribute to the development and maintenance of aggressive behavior.

Social Learning History

The long-term effects of a child's interactions with key people in his or her social environment also play a causal role in the development and maintenance of aggressive behavior. As already mentioned in Chapter 1, developmental life experiences play an important role in contributing to the aggressive behavior of youth. Patterson's developmental model (1982) clearly illustrates how historical factors, such as poor parental discipline and monitoring early in the child's life, give rise to antisocial behavior and low self-esteem.

Antisocial behavior acquired in early childhood gives rise to poor academic performance, parental rejection, peer rejection, and depression. These, in turn, lead to identification with a deviant peer group and subsequent delinquency. Finally, these life experiences set the stage for serious problems in adulthood, including disrupted marriages, chaotic employment, and possible incarceration or institutionalization. Along this developmental path, the child's aggressive behaviors are continuously shaped and maintained by immediate conditions that prevail in his or her social environment.

Contingencies in the Social Environment

A behavior approach to treatment is predicated on the notion that immediate conditions which are present in an individual's social environment give rise to the development and maintenance of behavior. Two central classes of conditions that exert a causal influence on behavior are antecedent and consequent events which are closely associated, in time, with the occurrence of behavior.

Antecedent Events

An antecedent event is a stimulus which indicates to a person that a certain behavior will either result in a favorable or unfavorable consequence. Antecedent events precede behaviors. For example, traffic lights are antecedent stimuli which signal particular driving behaviors. If the traffic light is green, it signals the driver to proceed. If it is red, it signals the driver to stop. The power of an antecedent stimulus to control behavior results from its association with the outcome or consequence of the behavior it evokes. Proceeding when the light is green is associated with safely negotiating an intersection, while stopping when the light is red is associated with the avoidance of an accident or other negative outcomes such as a traffic ticket or the anger of other drivers.

In regard to social behavior, such as aggression, the antecedent events which signal the occurrence of aggressive behavior are

associated with either a favorable outcome or the avoidance of an unpleasant consequence. These antecedents often are the behaviors of other people with whom the aggressive person interacts. For example, if a parent asks a child to clean his or her room, but the child is able to avoid the task by whining, then the parent's request becomes an antecedent event which signals to the child that whining will result in the avoidance of the task. This example presupposes that cleaning one's room is an unpleasant activity that the child wants to avoid. The parent's request will only become an antecedent event for whining if the parent discontinues the request when the child begins to whine. In this example, the parent's request has become an antecedent stimulus for whining because of the parent's inability to effectively discipline the child's whining (noncompliant) behavior. We can see, then, that the consequences which result from the behavior play a crucial role in determining the antecedents for aggressive behavior.

Consequent Events

Consequent events are the outcomes that result when a person engages in a behavior. Broadly speaking, behavioral consequences can be classified into two general types: reinforcing and punishing. Reinforcing consequences strengthen the behavior they follow and punishing consequences weaken the behavior they follow. In general, there are two types of reinforcing consequences and two types of punishing consequences.

Reinforcing Consequences

Reinforcing consequences follow a behavior and strengthen the probability that the behavior will occur again. There are two types of reinforcement: positive and negative.

Positive Reinforcement. Any event that follows a behavior and results in a pleasant outcome which strengthens the future occurrence of the behavior is a positive reinforcer.

There are many different positive reinforcers that parents or child-care staff can use to strengthen child and adolescent behavior. Some commonly employed positive reinforcers that can be used with children and adolescents are summarized in Figure 1.

The positive reinforcers listed in Figure 1 should not be thought of as an exhaustive list. It also should be remembered that what is considered to be a positive reinforcer for one person may not be a positive reinforcer for another. One way of determining positive reinforcers for a given child is to employ a reward survey. Reward surveys can be discussed with a child to determine which type of positive reinforcers could be employed to strengthen desirable behaviors. The reward survey (Figure 2) can help in determining individual positive reinforcers for a child.

Although positive reinforcers usually are employed to strengthen prosocial behavior (e.g. praising a youth for completing a task), they also can strengthen aggressive behavior. For example, a youth may get to watch a favorite TV show as a result of arguing with his or her parent about going to bed. Stealing snacks will result in a child obtaining a positive reinforcer by engaging in an anti-social behavior. Fighting with a sibling over a toy will result in positive reinforcement if the youth is able to obtain the toy through the aggression directed at the other youth. Positive reinforcers can strengthen either prosocial or aggressive behavior depending on which form of behavior produces the reward.

Negative Reinforcement. Many of the behaviors that a person engages in during the course of a day result in relief from, and avoidance of, unpleasant events. For example, buckling one's seat belt when starting a car allows the driver to terminate the noise of the seat belt buzzer and obtain relief from the irritating noise of the seat belt alarm. When a person opens an umbrella, this behavior allows the person to avoid the unpleasant experience of getting drenched by a downpour. Negative reinforcement is a procedure that involves the removal of an unpleasant event as a result of engaging in some behavior. For example, when a youth complies with a parental request so that his or her parents stop nagging, the youth's compliance behavior is negatively reinforced by the removal of the parents' nagging.

Like positive reinforcement, negative reinforcement strengthens behavior. In the example cited above, the youth is more likely to comply in the future when the parent nags because compliance was successful in stopping the parents' nagging. However, aggressive behaviors also can be negatively reinforced if they successfully terminate unpleasant events. Taking the same example of parental nagging, if the youth throws a temper tantrum which results in stopping the parents' nagging, then the youth's tantrumming behavior will be negatively reinforced and more likely to occur the next time the parents begin to nag. Patterson (1982) has found that parents of aggressive youth are more likely to give in to their youth's aggressive behavior because of an inability to effectively discipline the youth. In effect, parents are unknowingly strengthening aggressive behavior due to the operation of negative reinforcement.

FIGURE 1
COMMONLY USED POSITIVE REINFORCERS FOR CHILDREN AND YOUTH

1.	**Social:**	Praising, smiling, head-nodding, attention, touching, hugging, listening, spending time together, etc.
2.	**Consumable:**	Snacks, candy, juice, dining out, special meals, etc.
3.	**Activity:**	Watching TV, reading books, hobbies, movies, sports, having friends over, telephone time, etc.
4.	**Manipulative:**	Toys, blocks, puzzles, games, models, painting kits, records, etc.
5.	**Exchangeable:**	Stickers, stars, points, money, or other objects which can be exchanged for other reinforcers.

FIGURE 2
REWARD SURVEY

1. **People:** Who does the youth like to spend time with?

a. _____   b. _____

c. _____   d. _____

2. **Everyday Activities:** What everyday activities does the youth like to do? (For example: play Monopoly, roller-skate, watch TV, play puzzles, dolls, trucks)

a. _____   b. _____

c. _____   d. _____

3. **Special Activities:** What special activities does the youth enjoy? (For example: go to movies or the zoo, bake cookies, go to baseball game)

a. _____   b. _____

c. _____   d. _____

4. **Foods:** What are the youth's favorite foods and beverages?

a. _____   b. _____

c. _____   d. _____

5. **Attention:** What specific kinds of verbal and physical attention does the youth like? (For example: praise, compliments, hugs, pats on the back)

a. _____   b. _____

c. _____   d. _____

6. **Exchange Rewards:** What kind of exchange rewards (stars, tokens, money, happy faces) does the youth like to receive?

a. _____   b. _____

c. _____   d. _____

7. **Other Rewards:** List anything else the youth likes, is interested in, spends a lot of time doing, or would like to spend more time doing.

a. _____   b. _____

c. _____   d. _____

Punishment

Like reinforcement, there are two types of punishment which comprise the second category of consequent events: positive punishment and negative punishment (Hardy, 1988). Both forms of punishment work to weaken the behaviors they follow, decreasing the probability that these behaviors will recur in the future.

Positive Punishment. Positive punishment is the presentation of an unpleasant or aversive event following a behavior resulting in a weakening of the probability that the behavior will occur again. Positive punishers can take numerous forms, including yelling, scolding, lecturing, humiliating, hitting, frowning, criticizing, etc. Parents often will employ positive punishment to weaken various forms of child behavior. For example, spanking a child for pulling a cat's ears makes it less likely that the child will pull the cat's ears in the future. In this example, the parent presents an unpleasant event or stimulus (spanking) following the child's behavior (pulling the cat's ears), decreasing the future probability of the child repeating this behavior.

Children also can punish their parents' behavior. Let's say a parent asks a teenager to get off the phone. The teenager responds by screaming at the parent, "Get off my back." If the parent stops making requests of the teenager to get off the phone, then the teenager has effectively punished the parent for making these requests. The teenager presented an aversive stimulus (yelling at the parent) following a behavior (parental requests to get off the phone) that weakened or decreased its occurrence. It is interesting to note that the teenager's behavior (screaming at the parent) also has been negatively reinforced. The teenager engaged in a behavior (screaming) which turned off an aversive event to him or her (parental requests to get off the phone). Both the parent and teenager have been changed by the behaviors they exchanged with one another. The teenager learned to scream more often (negative reinforcement) when asked to get off the phone, and the parent learned not to ask the teenager to get off the phone any more (positive punishment) after making these requests. It is these kinds of interactions between family members which set the stage for the development of coercive behaviors in children and youth (Patterson, 1982).

Negative Punishment. Negative punishment is a special type of punishment resulting when something pleasant or positive is removed following a behavior. The result of taking away something positive from a person as a consequence of his or her behavior stops or weakens it. This form of punishment is referred to as response cost – a person's behavior (or response) ends up costing something valuable to him or her. Receiving a speeding ticket for driving too fast would be an example of negative punishment or response cost. The behavior of driving too fast results in the consequence of getting a ticket. The driver has to give up something he or she values; in this case, money in the form of a traffic fine. The traffic fine makes it less likely that the driver will continue to drive beyond the speed limit.

Parents and child-care providers can employ various events as negative punishers to weaken inappropriate child and youth behavior. One form of response cost is to remove certain privileges as a consequence for aggressive behavior. Forgatch (1988) suggests removing the following privileges:

Telephone usage, one day at a time
Television time
Transportation – car use, driving lessons, and rides to and from places
Bicycle, skateboard
Visiting with a friend
Stereo or radio use
Staying up late
Borrowing things that are taken for granted – clothes, tools, the hair dryer, etc.
Goodies in the refrigerator – ice cream, desserts, and cookies

Another method for employing response cost is Time Out. Time-Out can be used to decrease aggressive behaviors as well. time-out removes the child from a socially reinforcing situation. Forgatch (1988) has developed some excellent time-out rules that are depicted in Figure 3.

A third method for employing response cost is to impose a brief work chore as a consequence for an inappropriate behavior Forgatch (1988) has devised an eight-step procedure for using work chores as negative punishers, which is outlined in Figure 4.

The use of the Five-Minute Work Chore is most often used with adolescents as a consequence for noncompliant behavior.

The removal of privileges, the use of time-out, and the Five-Minute Work Chore are three examples of the types of consequences that can be used to decrease unwanted behavior via a response cost procedure. All three of these response cost procedures involve the removal of something the youth values as a consequence for negative behavior.

Patterson (1982) has found that the use of response cost is preferable to the presentation of aversives (positive punishment) as a method for disciplining aggressive behavior in children. Patterson has indicated that the presentation of aversives (yelling, scolding, sarcasm, etc.) is more likely to escalate aggressive behaviors in children. The use of response cost procedures are just as effective as positive punishment but are less likely to result in the escalation of aggressive behavior.

As stated earlier, the immediate consequences for behavior, along with key antecedent events, make up the contingencies which give rise to the occurrence, maintenance, and attenuation of behavior from moment to moment. The various forms of consequences that operate on behavior in the immediate social environment are summarized in Figure 5.

In order to understand aggressive behavior, it is important to analyze the function that aggressive behavior serves for the individual in his or her social environment. This form of behavioral assessment has been called a behavioral diagnosis, or functional analysis of behavior (Kanfer & Saslow, 1969).

The Functional Analysis Of Behavior

The assessment of aggressive behavior has traditionally relied on such tools as client interviews and self-report questionnaires. However, Patterson (1982) has found in his research with families who have aggressive children that these assessment tools have

FIGURE 3
TIME-OUT PROCEDURE

TIME-OUT
(Youth spends five minutes in a dull place for misbehavior.)

PLACE:

Select a dull, boring room where the door can be closed. The bathroom or laundry room are appropriate places. Inappropriate places are dark or frightening (e.g. closets), or entertaining (e.g. bedrooms, family rooms).

Prepare the room by removing delicate, dangerous, and entertaining objects (knick-knacks, cleaning fluids, books, toys).

PROCEDURE:

Use for one behavior, preferably noncompliance.

When the parent makes a request and the youth does not comply, use time-out.

Label the behavior and send the youth to time-out firmly, but calmly. Say: "Erik, that's not minding; go to time-out."

Set the timer for five minutes. When the bell rings, the youth may come out.

No conversations with the youth while in time-out.

Do not extract an apology afterwards. If the noncompliance was for a "stop" behavior ("Stop hitting your sister."), the incident is over. However, it may be necessary to begin the process again for start-up requests – "Get started on the dishes now." Calmly make the request again.

REFUSAL TO GO TO TIME-OUT:

Add one minute for each refusal, up to nine minutes total. Then say: "If you don't go to time-out right now, you will lose the following privilege (name the privilege)."

If the youth does not go at this point, time-out is dropped and the privilege is removed.

In preparing for time-out, generate a list of privileges to remove. Privileges removed should be small, important to the youth, brief, and something the parent can control.

CONTROL OF EMOTION:

Use time-out as soon as noncompliance occurs. Early intervention reduces anger for both parent and youth.

Role-play time-out. Pay attention to voice tone, body posture, facial expression.

If the youth misbehaves while in time-out, the parent needs another distraction: head phones, turn up the TV or radio, move to another area of the house, use telephone, learn and practice relaxation during this time.

Source: Forgatch, M. S. (1988). **A Social Learning Approach to Family Therapy**. Paper presented at the Taboroff Child and Adolescent Psychiatry Conference on Conduct Disorders in Children and Adolescents. Snowbird, UT; February 24-27.

FIGURE 4
THE FIVE-MINUTE WORK CHORE

EIGHT STEPS FOR USING THE FIVE-MINUTE WORK CHORE

1. Set the stage so you will not have to impose a work chore. This is done by creating a friendly atmosphere before making a request. It also is a good idea to time your request (if you can) so that it disrupts things as little as possible.

2. Warn the adolescent that you will impose a work chore as soon as your request is met with noncompliance. Keep in mind that your chances of success are better if you act right away.

3. Don't lecture or argue. A discipline encounter is not the time to discuss rationales, intentions, or the rights of adolescents. This may make you feel better, but adolescents are equipped with automatic switches that turn off their ears when there is evidence that a lecture is forthcoming. Arguing also defeats the cooling-off principle. It takes two to have an argument, so it is important for you to be strong enough to keep your mouth shut.

4. Each time you are about to make a request, have two work chores in mind that you can impose if necessary. You lose bargaining power when the situation arises and you can't think of a chore. Any of the routine household tasks are good, and picking weeds and other types of yard work also are favorites. A list of five-minute work chores that are commonly used by other parents is provided in Appendix A. Use this list as a starting point, but feel free to add chores that fit your situation.

5. Impose no more than two work chores before you withdraw a privilege. Once you withdraw the privilege, do not impose any more work chores. Privilege removal signals the end of the discipline confrontation; you will paint yourself and the adolescent into a corner if you add more chores.

6. Make sure the chore is brief. The chores you assign should be ones that you, or any other person, could complete in five minutes if you were working at a reasonable pace; that's where the "five-minute chore" got its name. Don't get involved in trying to prompt adolescents to hurry up while they are doing the chore. If it takes an hour to scour the kitchen sink, that's their problem. It shouldn't bother you.

7. Stay out of the way while they are doing the work. It is a rare teenager who can accept discipline with a smile. And it is a rare adult who doesn't have the urge to deliver a sarcastic or self-righteous comment about the justice of the work. Hostile interchanges at this point only disrupt the process. Don't tempt yourself – it is almost always better to stay away from the work area as much as you can until the chore is done.

8. Stay calm and neutral. Don't let the quality of your voice match that of your adolescent. You are the adult and you will be in control if you can avoid losing your temper. You only have to stay cool for a few minutes. If you can do that, you will win in the long run. Winning means teaching children that there will always be a consequence for noncompliance. Once they understand this, they realize it is easier to comply with your requests than it is to fight them. Whatever you do, stay calm.

Source: Patterson, G.R., & Forgatch, M.S. (1987). **Parents and Adolescents: Part I. The Basics.** Eugene, OR: Castalia Publishing Company.

FIGURE 5

BEHAVIORAL CONSEQUENCES AND THEIR EFFECTS ON BEHAVIOR

	Pleasant Event or Stimulus	Unpleasant Event or Stimulus
P r e s e n t i n g	TERM USED: Positive Reinforcement BEHAVIORAL RESULT: Acts to strengthen response EXAMPLES: Hugs, praise, points, etc.	TERM USED: Positive Punishment BEHAVIORAL RESULT: Weakens response or may terminate the response but is highly susceptible to side effects EXAMPLES: Reprimands, threats, corporal punishment, etc.
R e m o v i n g	TERM USED: Negative Punishment BEHAVIORAL RESULT: Weakens or terminates the response EXAMPLES: Loss of points, traffic ticket, time-out, etc.	TERM USED: Negative Reinforcement BEHAVIORAL RESULT: Acts to strengthen the response EXAMPLES: Turning off a loud radio, doing something that stops a baby from crying in church, etc.

limited value. His research led him to conclude that the assessment of aggressive behavior could be more reliably conducted through the direct observation of family interactions. This form of assessment involves observing the occurrence of aggressive behavior as it arises in social interaction. Specific attention is given to the antecedent and consequent events which are thought to cause aggressive behavior. This form of assessment has been called the functional analysis of behavior.

The goal of a functional analysis is to discover which environmental events are identified so they can be altered, causing a change in the behavior under assessment. In regard to aggressive behavior, the antecedent and consequent events that make up the contingencies which control aggressive behavior are most often the behavior of those individuals who interact with the aggressive child.

The following examples of aggressive behavior show how a functional analysis helps to identify and alter the contingencies which control aggressive behavior:

It's 9 p.m. and time for Reid to get to bed. His foster mom walks into the living room and announces "It's time for bed, Reid." Reid begins to whine and argue. Reid's foster mom sighs and says "Okay, you can stay up for a half hour more and then not another word out of you!"

In order to conduct a functional analysis of Reid's behavior, we must examine the antecedent and consequent events. This is done by laying out the sequence of events in the order in which they occurred.

The end result of this brief interaction is that Reid gets to continue watching TV. The foster mom also obtains relief from Reid's arguing and whining. Going back to the earlier discussion of consequent events, Reid's behavior acted as a punisher for the foster mom's request because it followed the mother's request and stopped it from recurring. When the foster mother "gave in" to Reid's whining, she obtained relief from his mildly aggressive behavior; negatively reinforcing her "giving in." In addition, on future occasions Reid is now more likely to whine and argue when given a request because the foster mom's "giving in" positively reinforced his whining and arguing.

Reid's behavior (arguing) was followed by an event (the foster mother's request) which was positive for Reid (getting to stay up later). The relations of the antecedent to consequent events surrounding Reid's behavior can be summarized as follows:

1. Reid's behavior punished the foster mom for making requests.
2. The foster mom's behavior of "giving in" was negatively reinforced because it turned off Reid's aggressive behavior.
3. Reid's behavior was positively reinforced by the foster mom "giving in" to it.

Based on our analysis of the antecedent and consequent events which surround Reid's behavior, it is easy to understand why the behavior is occurring. In order to change Reid's behavior, the antecedent and/or consequent events which surround it had to be changed. This could be done through the following arrangement:

Antecedent Events

It is 9 p.m. and time for Reid to get ready for bed. His foster mom walks into the TV room and annouces "It's time for bed, Reid."

Behavior

Reid begins to whine and argue.

Consequent Events

Reid's foster mom removes Reid's TV privileges for the next day and sends him to bed.

The end result of this set of interactions is that Reid stops arguing and goes to bed. Reid's arguing behavior has been effectively punished through the removal of a privilege (response cost) by the foster mom. The foster mom has been negatively reinforced by terminating Reid's arguing as a result of taking away his TV privilege. The foster mom also has been positively reinforced because removing Reid's TV privilege resulted in his going to bed. By changing the consequent event which followed Reid's behavior (the foster mom removing Reid's TV privilege), the following outcomes were obtained:

1. Reid's behavior was effectively punished by the foster mom.
2. The foster mom's use of response cost was negatively reinforced because it resulted in relief from Reid's whining and arguing.
3. The foster mom's use of response cost was positively reinforced because Reid went to bed.

How to Conduct a Functional Analysis of Behavior

The preceding examples show that a functional analysis of behavior can explain why a behavior is occurring and, at the same time, suggest ways of altering the behavior by adjusting environmental events. There are four steps to conducting a functional analysis of behavior:

1. Describe the contingencies which control a behavior. This involves specific descriptions of antecedent events, the behavior, and consequent events.
2. Arrange the descriptions of antecedent events, behavior, and consequent events into their proper sequence. This task can be easily done by using a functional analysis assessment sheet (Figure 6).
3. Analyze the antecedent and consequent events which control the aggressive behavior by determining punishers, negative reinforcers, and positive reinforcers for each person involved in the interaction.
4. Alter the antecedents and/or consequent events surrounding the problem behavior to bring about a change in the behavior.

In summary, the causes of aggressive behavior result from the interaction of three primary factors: inherited characteristics, the long-term effects of environmental contingencies which make up a person's individual social learning history, and the short-term effects of immediate social contingencies comprised of antecedent and consequent events. A person's behavior results from the simultaneous interaction of these three factors.

A functional analysis of behavior, which examines the antecedents and consequent events which control the development and maintenance of aggressive behavior, can be conducted to discover ways of altering aggressive behavior and changing contingencies in the child's current social milieu.

The skill-based workshop which accompanies this manual will give child-care providers an opportunity to learn and practice the skill of conducting a functional analysis of aggressive behavior.

FIGURE 6
FUNCTIONAL ANALYSIS ASSESSMENT SHEET

ANTECEDENT EVENT	BEHAVIOR	CONSEQUENT EVENT
Describe in detail the behavior of the person who interacted with the aggressive child just before the aggressive behavior occurred.	Describe in detail the child's aggressive behavior. Pay particular attention to body movements, facial expressions, and verbals.	Describe in detail the response of others in the child's immediate social environment. Pay particular attention to reactions and how he or she responds to aggressive behavior.

Chapter Three

Setting Boundaries For Aggressive Behavior

Generally, when one speaks of tolerance, it means a positive quality of a person who is open to and accepting of a wide variety of beliefs, ideas, and differences among people. When speaking of tolerance in terms of behaviors, however, one speaks of a fine line – or a tolerance level – which distinguishes between those behaviors one will or will not accept as appropriate. In the Boys Town Family Home Program, tolerance levels dictate when Effective Praise interactions are used (see "Relationship Development and Effective Praise" chapter) and when Teaching Interactions are used (see "Teaching Alternatives to Aggressive Behavior" chapter) to deal with appropriate and inappropriate behaviors of aggressive youth.

A high tolerance level means that a great deal of inappropriate behavior is accepted or tolerated, while a low tolerance level means that little inappropriate behavior is accepted or tolerated. It is critical for child-care staff to know that they can maintain low tolerance levels and still build positive relationships and function in society.

Aggressive youth are adept at raising the tolerance levels of adults. In fact, aggressive youth have been reinforced for raising the tolerance levels of adults because it gets their wants met (Patterson & Forgatch, 1987). The

following scenario between Bill (an aggressive youth) and his father illustrates this point:

Bill: "Would it be okay if I went over to Johnny's house to watch TV?"

Father: "No, not now, dinner is almost ready."

Bill: "Dad, I will only be gone a short time." (NOTE: Bill is now yelling and stomping his feet.)

Father: "No, Bill, now drop it!"

Bill: "I'm not going to stop asking until you let me go!" (NOTE: Bill shakes his fist at his father while making this statement.)

Father: "Get out of here, then, but don't be late for dinner."

In the above scenario, Bill was able to get what he wanted by yelling, stomping his feet, shaking his fist, and threatening his father. While Bill's father originally said "No" to Bill's request, Bill was able to raise his father's tolerance level (e.g. accepting Bill's inappropriate behavior when given a "No" answer) and was allowed to go to Johnny's house. Bill's inappropriate behavior has now been reinforced and is likely to occur again in the future. Having the knowledge and skills to effectively deal with the inappropriate behavior of aggressive youth will assist child-care staff in maintaining appropriate tolerance levels.

Importance of Low Tolerances

Inappropriate youth behavior is a sign that a youth does not know the **appropriate** behavior or skill to use in a given situation (e.g. Bill did not know the skill of accepting "No."). All youth have been told "No" to a request and have learned to engage in certain behaviors when this happens. Problematically for aggressive youth, these responses usually are dysfunctional; therefore, functional behavior must be taught. It is the responsibility of child-care staff to teach alternative skills when inappropriate behavior occurs. Tolerating inappropriate behavior sends a message to the aggressive youth that such behavior is acceptable. The acceptance of problem behaviors inadvertently reinforces and strengthens the behavior (as in the example with Bill). At best, the youth is confused about what is and what is not acceptable. At worst, failure to teach more appropriate skills means that aggressive youth are "set up" for failure in other settings because many adults in authority will not tolerate such problem behavior. In effect, aggressive youth are placed at greater risk when tolerance levels are high.

In addition to maintaining low tolerances, child-care staff are encouraged to strive for consistency in responding to the aggressive youth's appropriate or inappropriate behaviors. Consistency reduces the youth's confusion, helps demonstrate expectations, and makes it easier for him or her to learn and maintain appropriate skills. Consistency also will help to decrease the likelihood of tension and conflict between the child-care staff and the youth. The youth will perceive the child-care staff as being fair and reasonable, and positive relationships are more likely to develop and grow (Figure 1). By frequently talking to each other about the aggressive youth's progress, and by discussing any inconsistencies, child-care staff can work toward tolerance levels that are more consistent and fair.

Communicating Tolerance Levels

From the moment child-care staff begin working with an aggressive youth, they will be provided frequent opportunities to communicate their tolerance levels to the youth. The teaching procedures of the Boys Town Family Home Program (see "Relationship Development and Effective Praise," "Teaching Alternatives to Aggressive Behavior," "Preventing Aggressive Behavior," and "Crisis Intervention: The Short-Term Solution" chapters) provide child-care staff with specific, effective means of communicating their tolerance levels by emphasizing the importance of being pleasant, positive, and specific when interacting with youth.

Another way child-care staff communicate their tolerance levels to youth is through their own behavior or modeling. For example, periodically a child-care staff member will receive a "No" answer from his or her supervisor when requesting to do an activity with a youth. The staff member's response provides a behavioral example of his or her tolerance level for accepting "No" answers when he or she discusses the decision with the youth. By modeling the appropriate behavior, the staff member increases the likelihood that youth also will engage in the expected behavior.

Before child-care staff can adequately communicate their tolerance levels, a means for determining the appropriateness of the youth's behavior must be developed (Figure 2). The ability to observe and specifically describe verbal and nonverbal behaviors (see "Pinpointing Aggressive Behavior and Its Alternatives" chapter) is critical in determining the appropriateness of the youth's behavior.

As child-care staff set expectations for aggressive youth, they also need to understand how patience, encouragement, and recognition are combined with low tolerances to support these youth as they struggle to learn new ways of thinking and behaving. That is, child-care staff need to have low tolerances and high expectations, and recognize and praise the youth for any positive behavioral changes or efforts to master new skills. Low tolerances don't ensure that the youth's behavior will change rapidly. Aggressive youth have been repeatedly reinforced for behaving aggressively; therefore, it will take time to change their behavior. However, maintaining low tolerances, as defined by the social skills curriculum, helps adults to effectively and consistently communicate their expectations for these youth's skill performance and acquisition.

FIGURE 1
CONSISTENCY

RESULTS OF INCONSISTENT TOLERANCE LEVELS:

Confuses youth
Weakens treatment environment
Creates tension and conflict between adults
Creates tension and conflict between youth and adult
(hampers relationship development)

FIGURE 2
FACTORS IN DETERMINING THE APPROPRIATENESS OF YOUTH BEHAVIOR

Conflicts with societal norms
Breaks a rule in the program
Is physically harmful to any living being
Is an extreme emotional outburst
Causes discomfort or embarrassment to others
Jeopardizes the reputation of the program
Leads to negative consequences
Is not appropriate for the situation

Chapter Four

Pinpointing Aggressive Behavior And Its Alternatives

he foundation of effective teaching is the ability to recognize and describe behavior. Indeed, to use a functional analysis model to evaluate the aggressive youth's behavior (see "Assessing Aggressive Behavior in Children" chapter), child-care staff must possess excellent observing and describing skills. To observe and describe behavior, child-care staff must know what behaviors to observe, how to describe them, and how specificity enhances each component of the teaching procedures presented in this sourcebook. The ability to observe and describe behavior so that verbal and nonverbal behaviors are accurately specified also is critical in selecting skills an aggressive youth should be taught and in defining the behaviors that make up each skill. This chapter reviews the importance of specificity, how to describe behavior, what behaviors to observe, and how to use the ability to recognize and describe behavior to focus on skills when teaching.

Keys to Effective Behavioral Descriptions

In general, effective recognizing and describing skills involve the careful observation of antecedents, behaviors, and consequences, and the use of descriptions that are specific, objective, and behavioral. The descriptions are woven into the context of the Boys Town Family Home Program's teaching procedures, and are critical to the effectiveness and pleasantness of the teaching process. The following guidelines can help child-care staff effectively describe behavior. Effective descriptions of behavior: are specific, objective, and behavioral. Describing behavior effectively can be thought of as an instant verbal replay of behavior. This means that descriptions are worded so clearly that the behaviors could be repeated or reenacted by someone who had not originally made the observation. Such descriptions focus on observable events and behaviors that occur under a particular set of circumstances and avoid general or judgmental terms (e.g. "bad attitude," "good job," etc.).

Techniques for developing specific, behavioral descriptions include describing body language and movements, as well as verbal behavior. When describing verbal behavior, child-care staff can be most effective when they quote exactly what the youth said. If the child-care staff cannot offer an exact quote, the description can be preceded with the statement, "You said something like...." It also may be useful to demonstrate those behaviors that are particularly difficult to describe, such as voice tone and inflection. Such demonstrations can help aggressive youth understand the meaning of more subjective terms like "moody," "belligerent," etc. Child-care staff must demonstrate behavior in a helpful, concerned manner and be very careful to avoid mocking the youth. Of course, discretion must be used. Child-care staff should not repeat blatant sexual references, cursing, or racial slurs, etc. Without a helpful, matter-of-fact approach to the demonstration, the relationship could be damaged.

Finally, child-care staff will sometimes need to describe behaviors that did not occur but would have been appropriate for the situation; for example, the absence of eye contact when a youth is given an instruction, or not responding to a request for acknowledgment by saying "Okay" or "Sure."

In summary, child-care staff can most successfully describe behavior when they specifically, objectively, and behaviorally describe verbal and nonverbal behavior and avoid general or judgmental terms.

Benefits of Good Recognizing And Describing Skills

Good recognizing and describing skills make child-care staff more effective in teaching important behaviors. Recognizing and describing behavior helps make the aggressive youth aware of specific appropriate and inappropriate behavior. Vague or general descriptions such as, "You need to change your attitude" or "You have really been cooperative" do not help the youth learn exactly what behaviors need to be avoided or what behaviors should occur. Vague judgmental descriptions also can elicit argumentative behavior from the aggressive youth (e.g. "I do not have a bad attitude!" or "I do cooperate!"). Some examples of vague descriptions made more specific are listed in Figure 1.

FIGURE 1
VAGUE DESCRIPTIONS MADE SPECIFIC
EXAMPLES

VAGUE	SPECIFIC
Aggression	Shaking fists, raising voice, hitting, kicking, pointing finger in face
Temper tantrums	Crying, lying on the floor, kicking and pounding fists, throwing toys
Ungovernable	Stays out past curfew, takes the car without permission, yells at parents
Antisocial	Hits peers, spends all free time alone, argues with peers when playing games
Delinquent	Steals, carries weapons, has a juvenile record
Angry	Pounds fist on table, swears, walks away
Hostile	Says "Why are you always picking on me?" when given an instruction by parent

Clear behavioral descriptions further enhance teaching effectiveness by helping each youth understand what is expected. When expectations are clearly communicated, the youth is more likely to successfully learn skills. Success for the aggressive youth means that child-care staff can use their time more effectively and help the youth learn more skills.

Relationships between child-care staff and youth are enhanced through the skillful recognition and description of behavior. The use of specific, objective, and behavioral descriptions helps the child-care staff avoid judgmental terms that may damage an aggressive youth's self-esteem or trigger an emotional reaction (e.g. wrong, bad, stupid, terrible, a butt, a creep). When behavioral descriptions are clear, without being judgmental, aggressive youth are more likely to view the child-care staff as concerned, pleasant, and fair, and therefore, are more likely to be receptive to teaching. In fact, research has shown that youth prefer being told exactly how and what to do, and particularly rate specific, positive feedback as important (Willner et al., 1975).

What to Recognize And Describe

To determine what skills to teach (see Appendix B) and to most effectively use the teaching procedure components, child-care staff need to observe and describe antecedents, behaviors, and consequences.

When describing antecedent conditions, child-care staff need to know the circumstances surrounding the behavior. By reviewing who, what, when, and where, the child-

care staff can better determine whether the aggressive youth's behavior was appropriate or inappropriate and can more clearly identify the skill to teach or praise. Describing antecedents, behaviors, and consequences is a fairly straightforward process when the child-care staff actually observe or are involved in the interaction. However, on occasion they will need to rely on descriptions by others. When such occasions arise, the child-care staff need to ask specific questions in order to obtain as complete a picture as possible. The following section of this chapter reviews observations that need to be made by child-care staff or information needed to describe behavior and teach effectively.

Determining **who** is involved in the interaction is usually straightforward and can be quickly determined by observing or by asking the questions, "Who was involved?" and "Whom did the youth interact with?"

Determining **what** the conditions were immediately preceding the aggressive youth's behavior is the key to determining the skill to be taught or praised. By observing or asking what happened just before the youth's behavior, the child-care staff can describe the setting of events and identify the skill the aggressive youth needs to learn in order to be successful (e.g. "Was an instruction given?", "Was criticism given?", or "Did the youth receive a "No" answer?").

Reviewing **when** and **where** the behavior occurred also will help the child-care staff determine the type of intervention that should follow. If the behavior is appropriate for the time and place, child-care staff can reinforce and praise the youth. If it is inappropriate for the time or place, then child-care staff can teach a more appropriate response.

The antecedent conditions are reviewed in conjunction with the aggressive youth's behavior. Child-care staff need to know exactly what the youth was doing. That means being able to objectively describe body movements, facial expressions, and verbal behavior, as well as the intensity of these behaviors.

In terms of body movements, child-care staff need to describe large motor movements such as walking, sitting, standing, etc. They also need to describe small movements such as rolling of the eyes, a head nod, or crossed arms.

Facial expressions often are a key to how people perceive and react to one another. Therefore, child-care staff need to accurately describe to aggressive youth such relevant behaviors as eye contact when communicating with another person. Other examples of facial expression include smiling, frowning, squinting, etc.

In addition to describing the nonverbal behavior associated with body movement and facial expressions, child-care staff need to recognize and describe what is being said and how it is said. Repeating the specific words used by the aggressive youth and describing or demonstrating the tone of voice or inflection can help a youth gain a clearer understanding of his or her behavior. The specificity of the description will improve the aggressive youth's ability to change the behavior or to maintain the behavior if it is appropriate.

With respect to body movements, facial expression, and verbal behavior, child-care staff also may need to describe the frequency, intensity, and duration of those behaviors. Often, behaviors by themselves are neither appropriate nor inappropriate. The appropriateness of a behavior often relates to whether it

occurs frequently or not frequently enough, whether it escalates in intensity, or whether it goes on far too long or does not go on long enough. A demonstration of appropriateness by child-care staff can be very helpful here.

In addition to carefully recognizing and describing antecedents and behaviors, child-care staff need to be able to specify the consequences of the behavior. Analyzing the consequences can help the child-care staff formulate rationales for the youth and can help them understand the contingencies involved in maintaining, increasing, or decreasing the behavior. Observing the consequences of a behavior helps the child-care staff understand the contingencies that are reinforcing or maintaining certain behaviors. For instance, seeing an aggressive youth look away and not verbally respond when given an instruction, and then receive two additional instructions from the adult (consequence), can lead the child-care staff to conclude that attention may reinforce or maintain problem behaviors and noncompliance. Negative attention from adults (e.g. yelling and verbal threats) often acts as a consequence that maintains the inappropriate behavior of aggressive youth because the coercive interaction style they developed with their parents was based on negative attention. Whatever the consequences, they need not be described to the youth but should be used by staff in their analysis of behavior. The better a staff member understands contingencies and consequences, the better he or she can reorganize the environment to change the aggressive youth's behavior.

In summary, recognizing and describing antecedents, behaviors, and consequences improves the child-care staff member's ability to teach effectively. Descriptions of antecedents help determine the skill to be reinforced or the skill that needs to be taught. Accurate, objective descriptions of behavior help establish expectations and help ensure a successful and comfortable learning experience for the aggressive youth. Awareness of the natural and logical consequences helps the child-care staff understand the likelihood of the behavior occurring in the future as well as the contingencies that may have shaped the behavior in the past.

Building Skills

A beneficial way for child-care staff to determine the appropriateness of an aggressive youth's behavior, to set clear expectations, and to communicate their tolerance levels is through the use of a social skills curriculum. A social skills curriculum selected for use with aggressive youth is presented in Appendix B. A review of this curriculum illustrates that each social skill is delineated as a set of related behaviors. Research indicates that aggressive youth are deficient in the related behaviors associated with these social skills (Maerov, Brummett, Patterson, & Reid, 1978; Dishion et al., 1984; Patterson & Forgatch, 1987). The effectiveness of child-care staff in changing the aggressive youth's behavior, therefore, hinges on teaching these appropriate skill alternatives.

It is easy to see how labeling skills and describing specific behaviors within the context of teaching procedures has many advantages for aggressive youth and child-care staff. This makes the teaching process more efficient and more meaningful for the youth. The process is more efficient because several behaviors can be taught at the same time. The outcome is more meaningful and valuable to

the aggressive youth because it is easier for him or her to generalize the new skill to other settings or antecedent conditions. After all, an important goal of teaching an aggressive youth new ways of behaving is not only to have the youth learn something, but also to have the youth know when and where the new behaviors should be used.

Of the teaching procedures described in this manual, labeling skills and specifically describing behavior are most important in these teaching components: Initial Praise, Empathy or Affection; Description/Demonstration of the Inappropriate Behavior; Consequences; and Description/Demonstration of the Appropriate Behavior. Labeling and describing also are important when providing feedback after a youth practices a skill.

To assist child-care staff in understanding how descriptions of behavior and skill labeling fit into these four teaching components, an example is provided in Figure 2. Explanations related to the use of the component also are included.

In summary, the child-care staff can be pleasant, effective teachers by carefully recognizing and describing behavior using functional analysis, by labeling skills and describing the behaviors related to them, and by skillfully integrating these techniques into the components of the Teaching Interaction©.

FIGURE 2
SKILL-LABELING AND BEHAVIORAL DESCRIPTION

EXAMPLE

Situation: Chris is a new youth in the home and is watching TV. A child-care staff member asks Chris to help set the table. Chris sighs, doesn't look at the person, but gets up to walk to the kitchen. The use of the first four components might sound something like this:

1. INITIAL PRAISE, EMPATHY, OR AFFECTION
Example: "Chris, thanks for getting right up to come help set the table. I know it's hard to follow instructions sometimes, especially when you're enjoying watching TV."

Explanation: Specific, descriptive praise was given for "getting right up...." The general skill was identified in the context of the empathy statement, "I know it's hard to follow instructions...." Whenever possible, the initial praise should be related to behaviors that are part of the skill to be praised or taught.

2. DESCRIPTION/DEMONSTRATION OF THE INAPPROPRIATE BEHAVIOR
Example: "When I gave you that instruction, you sighed and you didn't look at me or say anything to let me know you heard or that you would help out."

Explanation: The skill label "instruction" is repeated and the description includes not only the inappropriate behavior of sighing, but also the absence of behaviors that would have been appropriate (e.g. "You didn't look at me or say anything...."). Also note that the staff member avoids vague and judgmental descriptions such as "You weren't very cooperative..." or "You didn't seem too happy when asked you to...."

3. CONSEQUENCES
Example: "Please take out your point card and give yourself 1,000 negative points for not following instructions. You'll have a chance to earn some of the points back by practicing how to follow instructions."

Explanation: The use of the consequence provides an opportunity to very clearly and concisely label the skill that is the focus of the interaction and to indicate that practicing the skill will enable the youth to earn back some of the points. Note: Child-care staff should be sure to use phrases like "Give yourself..." or "You've earned..." when delivering consequences, rather than "I'm taking away..." or "I'm going to give you...." The former phrasing helps the youth understand that he or she owns the behavior and is responsible for the consequences – not the child care staff. The negative consequences help decrease the probability that such problem behavior will occur in the future.

4. DESCRIPTION/DEMONSTRATION OF THE APPROPRIATE BEHAVIOR
Example: "Chris, let's talk about following instructions. Whenever anyone gives you an instruction, whether it's a teacher, your parents, or an employer, there are several things you need to do. You need to look at the person and answer them by saying 'Okay' or 'Sure' or something to let the person know you're listening and will follow through. Do the task and then check back with the person when you're done."

Explanation: The child-care staff member helps the youth generalize to other situations by explaining the antecedent condition, "Whenever anyone gives you an instruction...." Then the staff member provides a clear, step-by-step, behavioral description to help the youth lean the skill. During a real interaction, the staff member should pause frequently to ask the youth if he or she understands, has any questions, etc.

42

Chapter Five

Relationship Development And Effective Praise

Aggressive youth have developed an interaction style that is punishing to family, peers, and other adults. They have been inadvertently taught by their families to be abrasive (verbally and sometimes physically) toward others to get what they want (Patterson & Forgatch, 1987). Therefore, aggressive youth have difficulty developing and maintaining positive relationships. Because these youth approach all relationships similarly, their difficulty with developing positive relationships is not limited to family members. Yet, nurturing relationships are a key to a rewarding and happy life. Positive relationships between child-care staff and the aggressive youth they work with are critical if these youth are to benefit from their experiences with child-care staff.

This section will explore the benefits of strong relationship development in remediating aggressive youths' behavior, and present several techniques to enhance relationship development.

Benefits of Building Strong Relationships

There are numerous benefits for developing and maintaining strong, personal relationships with every youth. But developing positive relationships with aggressive youth is particularly important. In general, strong relationships between child-care staff and youth enhance the staff's ability to help bring about change in each youth's life and create a more pleasant living environment. Strong relationships contribute substantially to the child-care staff's ability to help each youth learn and grow (Braukmann, Kirigin, & Wolf, 1976). When relationships are healthy and strong, the youth are more likely to spend time with the child-care staff. When youth seek out child-care staff and want to be with them, the entire teaching and learning process is greatly enhanced. Child-care staff have many more opportunities to teach by example as youth spend more time in the presence of positive, adult role models. As relationships develop, the youth also are more likely to identify with and accept the values, rationales, and opinions expressed by the child-care staff. Furthermore, children are more likely to emulate the behaviors, values, and morals of adults with whom they have good relationships (Hirschi, 1969; Raz, 1977).

Not only is the effectiveness of the child-care staff's role-modeling improved due to good relationships, but the youths' receptivity to more direct teaching also is improved. That is, youth are more likely to accept the child-care staff's feedback, whether it takes the form of a compliment or a complete Teaching Interaction to correct an inappropriate behavior. Therefore, relationship development impacts positively on some critical behavior problems of aggressive youth (Appendix B). For example, they can be taught crucial skills, such as "following instructions" or "accepting criticism" more readily. Such skills not only help the youth learn other skills (e.g. they have to be able to follow instructions and accept criticism before they can be taught other skills) but also make the youth more pleasant to be around.

Aggressive youth not only need the benefit of positive role models and active help through teaching, but also to be able to talk with child-care staff about how they are feeling and what they are thinking. With sensitive relationships to rely on, these youth are much more likely to communicate frequently and honestly. With frequent, open communication, child-care staff are better able to be sensitive to the needs of each youth and better able to individualize treatment to best help the youth.

Positive relationships with staff also help aggressive youth develop other positive relationships. As youth develop close ties to child-care staff, they begin to care about the child-care staff's opinions of them. In essence, the child-care staff's approval and view of the youth become reinforcers for the youth. Aggressive youth slowly learn and adopt nonabrasive ways (e.g. disagreeing appropriately, accepting "No" answers, and asking permission) of dealing with people as their positive relationships with child-care staff enable them to learn new skills, thus helping the youth break their coercive style of inter-

acting with authority figures (Patterson et al., 1984). Over time, these youth come to care about the opinions and approval of important role models and significant others such as clergy, teachers, and family. The skills they have been taught by child-care staff allow them to develop positive relationships with these groups as well. Since the coercive interpersonal style learned in the home by aggressive youth generalizes to the school setting, aggressive youth have difficulties getting along with their peers (Patterson, Dishion, & Bank, 1984). Positive relationships with child-care staff work, through modeling and skill acquisition, to help aggressive youth develop positive relationships with their peers. In addition, the more closely the youth identify with the child-care staff, the less likely they are to be negatively influenced by their peers – a common problem for aggressive youth (Freedman, Rosenthal, Donahue, Schlundt, & McFall, 1978). Drugs, illegal activity, and acts of defiance are more likely to be resisted by youth who feel close to their child-care staff.

How Relationships Develop

Relationships do not develop over the course of a few days or months. Nor can a relationship ever be considered "developed." Rather, a relationship can be viewed as continually developing over time and across the events and issues that arise as people interact with one another. Relationships, positive or negative, begin to develop as a result of people interacting with others around common experiences or interests. Strong, positive relationships grow because people have mutually enjoyable or compatible behaviors, qualities, or values, and because they interact with each other in a pleasant and friendly fashion. Child-care staff begin developing positive relationships with aggressive youth by finding out about the youth's interests and spending time involved in activities of mutual interest.

Generally speaking, there is a common set of behaviors and attitudes that are both socially acceptable and generally valued by members of society that relate to relationship development. These behaviors and values include such concepts as honesty, sensitivity, concern for others, a sense of humor, reliability, willingness to listen, etc. In essence, these behaviors and values can be conceptualized as skills that help build positive relationships. With these skills, people are able to develop positive relationships with each other. When child-care staff use these skills during interactions with aggressive youth, they set the tone for building positive relationships.

Quality Components: Skills That Help Develop Relationships

While the teaching procedures described in this sourcebook can build relationships, it also would be possible to engage in such "procedural" components and not build relationships. The use of such teaching procedures must be accompanied by quality components as well. Quality components refer to the positive verbal and nonverbal behavior of the child-care staff that accompany the use of the procedural components. Such quality components include looking at the youth, answering the youth's questions, having a pleasant facial expression, appropriately using humor, appropriately using physical contact such as

hugs or an arm around the shoulder, etc. Research conducted by Willner et al. (1975) indicates that youth can clearly describe child-care staff behaviors they like and dislike, and supports the importance of quality components in relationship development (Figure 1).

How to Assess Relationships

Even though child-care staff are helping aggressive youth learn how to develop positive relationships by teaching important skills, assessing the relationship development between child-care staff and these youth is essential (Figure 2). When a weak relationship is noted, it signals the need for the child-care staff to evaluate their interactions with the youth. Requesting feedback from other staff members on dimensions such as concern, pleasantness, and praise for accomplishments will assist the child-care staff in developing a strategy to strengthen the relationship.

Effective Praise

Helping Aggressive Youth Learn To Develop Relationships

Aggressive youth have not developed positive relationship-building skills because, by definition, the abrasive behaviors they have effectively used to get their needs met are the direct alternatives of positive relationship-building behaviors. They need to learn certain skills that make them more attractive to others and allow them to develop positive relationships. It is the child-care staff's responsibility to teach aggressive youth the skills they need in order to develop positive relationships with adults and peers. Some of these skills are listed in Figure 3.

FIGURE 1
LIKED AND DISLIKED BEHAVIORS

LIKED BEHAVIOR	DISLIKED BEHAVIOR
Calm, pleasant voice tone	Describing only what the youth did wrong
Offering or providing help	Anger
Joking	Negative feedback
Positive Feedback	Profanity
Fairness	Lack of understanding
Explanation of how or what to do	Unfriendly
Explanation of why (giving reasons)	Unpleasant
Concern	Bossy, demanding
Enthusiasm	Unfair consequences
Politeness	Bad attitude
Getting right to the point	Unpleasant physical contact
Smiling	Mean, insulting remarks
	No opportunity to speak
	Shouting
	Accusing, blaming statements
	Throwing objects

FIGURE 2
RELATIONSHIP ASSESSMENT

STRONG RELATIONSHIP	WEAK RELATIONSHIP
The youth spends a lot of his or her free time around the child-care staff.	The youth spends little or no free time around the child-care staff.
The youth engages in behaviors that he or she knows pleases the child-care staff (e.g. says "Please" and "Thank you" to the staff, brings the staff member a birthday card).	The youth usually fails to engage in behaviors he or she knows pleases the child-care staff.
The youth volunteers to help the child-care staff in some way even through no positive consequences are associated with volunteering.	The youth rarely volunteers to help the child-care staff and only volunteers if he or she expects a consequence.
The youth routinely makes positive comments about the child-care staff to other youth and adults.	The youth routinely makes negative or inappropriate comments about the child-care staff to other youth and adults.

FIGURE 3
RELATIONSHIP-BUILDING SKILLS

EXAMPLES

Following Instructions: The youth is able to look at the person giving the instructions, acknowledge the instruction, do what is requested immediately without arguing or talking back, and then let the person know the task if finished.

Accepting "No" for an Answer: The youth is able to look at the person, acknowledge the answer without arguing, whining, or making threatening statements, remain calm, and only later appropriately disagree.

Making a Request (Asking a Favor): The youth is able to look at the person, ask the question in a clear pleasant voice tone, and say "Thanks" if the answer is "Yes" or engage in the skill of accepting "No" for an answer if the request is denied.

Accepting Criticism or a Consequence: The youth is able to look at the person giving the criticism, acknowledge the criticism, and not argue.

When teaching aggressive youth relationship-building skills, it is especially important to apply the teaching procedure of Effective Praise. Effective Praise is crucial to developing relationships and is very important in strengthening appropriate behavior of the aggressive youth (Patterson & Forgatch, 1987). Effective Praise interactions allow the child-care staff to sincerely and enthusiastically recognize the progress the aggressive youth is making to learn appropriate ways of interacting with others. When the youth engages in an appropriate social skill that is the alternative to his or her usual aggressive response (e.g. accepting "No" versus having a temper tantrum) the youth's appropriate behavior should be recognized. In the Boys Town Family Home Program, Effective Praise consists of five components or steps (Figure 4).

FIGURE 4
EFFECTIVE PRAISE STEPS

1. Praise
2. Description of Appropriate Behavior
3. Rationale
4. Request for Acknowledgment
5. Positive Consequences

The steps of Effective Praise work together to provide child-care staff with a means of clearly communicating concern for youth, as well as their approval and appreciation when the youth is behaving appropriately and making strides to change specific aggressive behaviors. The steps of Effective Praise are:

Praise: The child-care staff member begins the interaction on a positive note by praising the youth for some appropriate behavior. The praise should be specific and genuine.

Example: "Sarah, you really did a nice job of following instructions."

Description of Appropriate Behavior: The staff member specifically describes the youth's appropriate verbal and nonverbal behavior. This step begins by describing the antecedent. Antecedents are conditions that occur prior to a behavior. They help set the stage for certain responses.

Example: "When you received that criticism...," "When I gave you the instruction to...," or "When you asked for help...."

Rationale: The staff member provides the aggressive youth with a reason for continuing to behave appropriately. The rationale should be youth-oriented to help the youth internalize what they are learning and help motivate them to change.

Example: "By following instructions right away you will have more free time to spend having fun."

Request for Acknowledgment: The staff member requests acknowledgment to make sure that the youth understands what is being said. Requests for acknowledgment take the form of a question.

Example: "Do you understand?", "Does that make sense to you?", or "Do you know what that means?"

Positive Consequences: The staff member gives positive consequences as a reward for the appropriate behavior, and to increase the likelihood of the behavior recurring. Positive consequences can take the form of privileges, activities, material objects, etc.

Example: "For accepting 'No,' you've earned a half-hour TV show tonight," or "You may play basketball for an hour this evening," or "You've earned a new comic book."

Figure 5 gives examples of Effective Praise interactions using all five steps. The social skills illustrated in the examples (e.g. "following instructions" and "accepting criticism") are typically deficient in aggressive youth (Patterson, 1982).

FIGURE 5
EFFECTIVE PRAISE INTERACTIONS

FOLLOWING INSTRUCTIONS

Praise

"Mary, you really did a nice job of following that instruction."

Description of Appropriate Behavior

"When I gave you the instruction to make your bed you looked at me and said, 'Okay, I'll do that right away.' You made your bed, and after you finished making your bed you let me know you were done."

Rationale

"By following instructions from people right away, you don't waste your time. That way you have more free time to spend doing fun things like riding your bike."

Request for Acknowledgment

"Do you understand what I mean?"

Positive Consequences

"For following instructions Mary, you have earned 15 minutes of phone time."

ACCEPTING CRITICISM

Praise

"Joe, that was great and so impressive. You have really come a long way in learning to accept criticism.

Description of Appropriate Behavior

"When we reviewed the problem behaviors that were listed on your school note you really handled it well. You looked at me as we talked, you calmly explained what happened, and you didn't argue, raise your voice or make excuses. Superb!"

Rationale

"By accepting criticism that way, you can learn a lot and you can avoid creating more problems. I know that you are really looking forward to playing basketball, but I'm sure the coach will need to criticize your playing to help you improve. If you can handle his feedback as well as you've handled this criticism, you'll probably spend more time playing and less time on the bench."

Request for Acknowledgment

"Does that make sense?"

Positive Consequences

"Why don't you go ahead and play basketball outside until I call you for dinner."

In summary, there will be many benefits from using praise effectively and consistently with aggressive youth. First, it is a powerful teaching tool that is easy for child-care staff to use to reinforce a youth's appropriate behavior. Second, by pointing out the specific positive behavior a youth has demonstrated and complimenting him or her for it, the chances of that behavior occurring again increases. These positive behaviors will allow the aggressive youth to develop positive relationships and experience success with adults and peers. Third, as the frequency of positive behaviors increases, the aggressive behaviors decrease. Fourth, by focusing on positive behaviors makes the child-care staff's time with each youth more pleasant and helps build positive relationships. Fifth, consistently complimenting the youth for positive behaviors will improve his or her self-concept by giving him or her a stronger sense of accomplishment (Figure 6).

FIGURE 6
BENEFITS OF EFFECTIVE PRAISE

1. Powerful teaching tool.

2. Increases likelihood of appropriate behavior in the future.

3. Occurrence of inappropriate behavior decreases.

4. Helps build positive relationships.

5. Enhances youth's self-concept.

Chapter Six

Teaching Alternatives To Aggressive Behaviors

Aggressive youth have had a difficult time being successful in their families, their schools, and their communities. They have lived in dysfunctional and often chaotic environments. As a result, they have presented difficulties and exhibited problem behaviors that may have resulted in labels such as "delinquent," "antisocial," or "ungovernable."

Along with their problems, each aggressive youth also has special strengths and qualities. The goal of the Boys Town Family Home Program is to build on each youth's strengths and to remedial problems. Rather than viewing an aggressive youth as delinquent or ungovernable, child-care staff take the approach that youth need to learn a wide variety of skills. Most youth learn societal norms and appropriate behaviors and skills by observing and emulating the many positive role models available to them. The aggressive youth whom child-care staff work with have not had the benefit of positive, consistent role models; instead, role models have tended to be harsh in their discipline practices (Farrington, 1978) and inconsistent as well (McCord et al., 1959). Often their "reinforcement histories" have led the youth to develop behaviors that provide them immediate gratification, but in the long run are very self-destructive.

Because these youth have so much to learn and "unlearn" in a relatively short time, frequent, direct, and skillful teaching is the key to success. Teaching is the critical difference between real treatment and mere caretaking. Child-care staff can help each aggressive youth learn new skills that are alternatives to past problem behaviors (e.g. accepting "No," disagreeing appropriately, etc.) and promote his or her normal developmental progress through adolescence. Because aggressive youth are actively taught new ways of behaving, each youth can more successfully and comfortably adapt to societal norms to get his or her needs met in socially acceptable ways.

In the Boys Town Family Home Program, years of study and research have been devoted to the question of what constitutes effective teaching. It is clear that each individual's style of interacting is the most powerful factor in determining the effectiveness of his or her teaching. People who are perceived as warm, energetic, considerate, positive, concerned, and genuine are usually highly effective in any interaction, if just for the mere fact that they are enjoyable to be with. It is very fortunate that people who want to be child-care staff usually possess these qualities because it is difficult to teach people how to be genuine, warm, etc. The behaviors that lead to describing a person as "warm," for example, are not only difficult to define in objective, teachable terms, but also appear to be learned through a variety of experiences that are not easily replicated in a training workshop environment. There are, however, observable behaviors that are generally associated with certain positive personality styles. These behaviors are referred to as **quality components** of teaching and include such behaviors as pleasant facial expressions, gestures or statements of affection, humor, body positions, and calm voice tones. The degree to which child-care staff incorporate these behaviors into their teaching determines to a large degree how well a youth will respond to the content of what is being taught. These quality components are especially important to use when correcting aggressive youths' behavior as they were usually lacking in their parents' discipline style (Farrington, 1978).

Direct, frequent, concerned teaching also helps child-care staff. This teaching approach provides a specific, effective, positive way to deal with problem behaviors. Because teaching is a positive approach that works well and is liked by youth, child-care staff can avoid punitive approaches that would damage relationships. For example, Bedlington, Solnick, Braukmann, Kirigin, and Wolf (1979) evaluated several group homes and found that the level of teaching in a home was positively correlated with youth satisfaction and negatively correlated with self-reported delinquency. That is, the more teaching done by the child care staff, the better the youth liked the program and the less delinquency they reported. Since many of the delinquency variables reported are associated with aggressive youth, it would seem reasonable to assume that child-care staff working with aggressive youth would achieve the same results.

In the Boys Town Family Home Program, a process for effectively teaching alternatives to inappropriate youth behavior has evolved over the past 15 years. This process is known as the **Teaching Interaction**. To most effectively and sensitively meet the individual needs of each aggressive youth, child-care staff should consistently use Teaching Interactions. The Teaching Interaction is a nine-step process for dealing with a youth's problem behaviors and teaching more appropriate alternatives. By mastering and thoughtfully using the components of the Teaching Interaction, child-care staff can help each aggressive youth recover from the past and grow into the future.

The remainder of this chapter reviews in more detail each of the nine components of the Teaching Interaction (Figure 1). In addition, some special techniques and applications are reviewed to help child-care staff successfully apply their teaching skills.

Teaching Interaction Components

The following nine components and the various subcomponents are utilized to correct problem behaviors of aggressive youth and teach new alternative skills and behaviors. These components are listed, defined, and reviewed on the following pages.

Initial Praise, Empathy, or Affection

Each interaction begins on a positive note by providing specific, sincere praise that describes aspects of the youth's behavior that are appropriate. To make such praise most effective it should be behaviorally specific and descriptive (see "Pinpointing Aggressive

FIGURE 1
TEACHING INTERACTION

---

1. Initial Praise, Empathy, or Affection
2. Description/Demonstration of Inappropriate Behavior
3. Consequences
    – Negative Consequence
    – Positive Correction Statement
4. Description/Demonstration of Appropriate Behavior
5. Rationale
6. Request for Acknowledgment
7. Practice
8. Feedback
    – Praise
    – Specific Description or Demonstration
    – Positive Consequences
9. General Praise

Behavior and Its Alternatives" chapter) and it should be related to the skill that will be taught or to an approximate behavior. The descriptive, specific nature of the praise serves to further increase the probability that those appropriate behaviors will occur again. Praising behavior related to the skill has two functions. First, it increases the sincerity and naturalness of the teaching. Second, it reinforces approximations to the desired behavior and helps the youth recognize progress.

If the youth is not engaging in behavior that warrants praise or appropriate behavior related to the skill to be taught, the child-care staff member can still begin the Teaching Interaction on a positive note by providing an empathy statement. An empathy statement lets the youth know that the staff member understands how she or he may be feeling.

Example: "Mark, I know how much you were counting on going to the concert and I'm sure you're really disappointed that you can't go" or "It is really irritating when somebody breaks your bike and doesn't tell you about it."

Such empathy statements can help build relationships, calm an agitated youth, and help the staff member approach the situation in a positive, relaxed manner.

Initial praise and empathy also can be accompanied by verbal and nonverbal expression of affection. Affection is an important quality component that can be conveyed by a concerned, pleasant tone of voice, a comforting hand on the shoulder, a pat on the back, a smile, or a statement of care and concern (e.g. "Mary, I'm really concerned about you."). Such expressions of affection enhance the overall quality of the praise or empathy and let the youth know that it is only his or her behavior that is an issue – not the relationship with the child-care staff. (See "Relationship Development and Effective Praise" chapter.)

Without the consistent use of this component, the aggressive youth may come to view the staff member as a punishing stimulus – someone who is quick to criticize and slow to recognize accomplishments. Based on the learning history of aggressive youth when they have received criticism (e.g. harsh, unpleasant discipline), it is likely they already see Corrective Teaching as punishing.

With the consistent use of initial praise, empathy, and affection, the child-care staff can strengthen and reinforce appropriate behavior. They can build relationships by recognizing accomplishments, acknowledging feelings, and they can help the aggressive youth be more receptive and open to the entire teaching process and come to view Corrective Teaching as pleasant, not punishing.

Description/Demonstration Of Inappropriate Behavior

This component involves labeling the skill that will be taught and specifically describing the aggressive youth's inappropriate verbal and nonverbal behavior. Labeling the skill often is accomplished by describing the antecedent conditions.

Example: "When you asked for permission...," or "When I gave you the instruction to...."

When behaviors are difficult to describe, such as voice tone, gestures, or facial expressions, the child-care staff may demonstrate the behavior so the youth specifically understands the problem that should be corrected.

Child-care staff will want to be sure to use the skills learned in the "Pinpointing Aggressive Behavior and Its Alternatives" chapter to provide clear skill labels and non-judgmental, specific behavioral descriptions. Specific descriptions of inappropriate behaviors help the aggressive youth understand exactly what behaviors need to be changed. He or she is not left trying to guess about the meaning or interpret vague terms such as "attitude," "defiant," or "aggressive." Descriptions of inappropriate behavior also help the youth understand the tolerance levels and limits of the child-care staff.

Without clear, objective descriptions of inappropriate behavior, an aggressive youth will remain unaware of what behaviors are inappropriate and continue to behave inappropriately.

To be most effective, such descriptions or demonstrations of behavior need to be delivered in a matter-of-fact, calm manner. Child-care staff need to be especially careful not to use harsh or accusing voice tones and not to mock the youth or exaggerate their behaviors. A calm, matter-of-fact approach makes it more likely that the youth will listen and learn. A belittling, harsh, or mocking approach is likely to result in an emotional reaction, and potentially, a confrontation.

In summary, clear skill labels and specific behavioral descriptions of inappropriate behavior delivered in a calm, matter-of-fact manner can help the aggressive youth quickly learn expectations and behaviors that need to be changed.

Consequences

This component involves delivering applied negative consequences; for example, the loss of a privilege for the inappropriate behaviors. Immediately following the consequence, the staff member offers a positive correction statement. A positive correction statement lets the aggressive youth know that he or she will have an opportunity to immediately earn some of the consequences back by practicing the skill or behavior that resulted in earning negative consequences.

Example: "For not accepting criticism you have lost 30 minutes of television time. You'll have a chance to earn some of that consequence back by practicing."

Up to half of the consequences lost may be earned back during the practice session.

When delivering the consequence, the staff member takes the opportunity to re-label the skill (e.g. "You've lost privileges for not asking permission."). The staff member also makes sure to use phrases such as "You've earned..." or "You've lost..." rather than "I'm giving you..." when delivering consequences. Using the former phrases helps the youth understand that it is his or her behavior that has resulted in a consequence – not the behavior of the staff member.

The negative consequence and the positive correction statement also should prompt the staff member to remember the "4:1 Rule" regarding positive correction. The "4:1 Rule" means that for any misbehavior for which a youth loses a privilege, the child-care staff should provide at least four opportunities during that day for the youth to practice the alternative positive behavior and earn positive consequences. Since aggressive youth have received few positive consequences for their pro-social behavior, child-care staff should make every effort to provide at least four pos-

itive consequences for every negative consequence.

Immediate, calm delivery of negative consequences along with a positive correction statement helps discourage the aggressive youth from engaging in the inappropriate behavior in the future and helps motivate him or her to learn a new skill. Without the use of negative consequences, child-care staff may actually reinforce the inappropriate behavior with their attention, teaching, and concern. The negative consequence provides a response cost to the aggressive youth for engaging in the inappropriate behavior.

Description/Demonstration Of the Appropriate Behavior

Following the consequence, the child-care staff describes to the youth the appropriate behavior that should replace the inappropriate behavior. This gives the aggressive youth an alternative behavior or skill to use in the future. The effective use of this component is similar to the effective use of the description/demonstration of the inappropriate behavior. That is, it involves labeling the skill and specifically describing the desired verbal and nonverbal behavior. Like the description of the inappropriate behavior, the staff may choose to model the behaviors that make up the skill. They also help the aggressive youth generalize the skill to other situations by explaining relevant antecedent conditions.

Example: "Whenever someone has to tell you "No," whether it's your parents or a teacher, here's what you should do..." or "Whenever you answer the telephone...."

Such descriptions of antecedent conditions not only help the youth generalize the skill, but also are supportive to the youth because he or she will come to understand that the teaching will benefit him or her in many situations and is not an arbitrary process. Descriptions of appropriate behavior also can be made more supportive and non-judgmental by avoiding "I" statements such as "I want you to...." Phrases such as "What you should do..." or "Next time you can try to..." sound less judgmental, yet clearly tell the child what behaviors need to occur in the future.

Clear skill labels, along with specific, step-by-step behavioral descriptions, make it more likely that an aggressive youth will successfully learn new ways of behaving and help the staff teach effectively and pleasantly.

Rationale

A rationale is a statement explaining to the youth the natural consequences for his or her behavior. Youth view child-care staff as more concerned and fair when they point out the benefits of learning a new skill or the benefits of continuing to behave appropriately (Willner et al., 1975). Short-term, individualized rationales help aggressive youth internalize what they are learning and help motivate them to change. Rationales also provide child-care staff with an excellent means to teach morals and values, and should be extended to include sensitivity to others.

Example: "Stealing not only causes more problems but also hurts others."

Request for Acknowledgment

Requests for acknowledgment occur frequently throughout the teaching process. The child-care staff member frequently checks with the youth to be sure that he or she under-

stands what is being said. These requests for acknowledgment take the form of questions.

Example: "Do you understand?", "Do you have any questions?", or "Can you repeat that back to me?"

Requesting acknowledgment promotes a dialogue and helps avoid lecturing. It also lets the child-care staff know how well they are teaching and how much the aggressive youth is understanding.

To effectively use this component, the child-care staff must not only request acknowledgment but also be sure the youth verbally responds to the request – preferably in brief but complete sentences. In addition, the child-care staff must continually look at their own behavior to make sure they are providing time for the youth to acknowledge by pausing after asking for acknowledgment. Child-care staff also must be clear that they are not necessarily asking the aggressive youth if he or she agrees with what is being said, but rather if he or she understands what is being said. Avoiding requests for acknowledgment that promote disagreement or arguing will facilitate the teaching process. For example, child-care staff should avoid requests for acknowledgment such as, "Don't you agree?" or "How do you feel about that?" Such requests for input are more appropriate for counseling sessions.

Frequent requests for acknowledgment help child-care staff avoid lecturing and provide an opportunity for youth to productively participate in the learning process. Therefore, requests for acknowledgment should occur often but always after a rationale has been given to ensure that the aggressive youth understands the benefit of learning the skill.

Practice

During the practice portion of the teaching, the youth has the opportunity to actually demonstrate the skill the staff member has just taught. This component is one of the most powerful and important aspects of teaching. These practice sessions provide the aggressive youth with the opportunity to develop new habits and to become comfortable with new ways of behaving before he or she needs to use the skill again in a real setting. This artificial practice session also provides important information for the child-care staff. It is the only way a staff member can assess the effectiveness of his or her teaching. Over time, staff members can become better teachers by closely observing the success of aggressive youth during practice sessions and then making the necessary adjustments in their teaching skills to be more effective.

Practice sessions can be most effective and most successful for the youth when they are clearly set up with specific instructions to the youth. For instance, the child-care staff will need to clearly "set the stage" by describing the setting and antecedent conditions and by reviewing the behaviors the aggressive youth needs to engage in during the practice.

Example: "Okay Mark, we are going to practice how to accept 'No.' I'll walk into the room and you'll ask me if you can go to the movies. I'll say 'No,' and then you'll look at me, say "Okay...."

Sometimes, practice sessions can be more successful if a similar, but hypothetical, situation is used. This can be particularly helpful if the original inappropriate behavior involved an emotional or intense response by the youth. In such situations the child-care staff may set up a realistic practice that involves using the new skill but does not involve the original situation. For example, a youth has been told that he will not be able to attend a concert and has responded by swearing and arguing. While teaching the youth how to accept "No" for an answer, the staff member would probably have the youth first practice the skill by using a pretend issue (e.g. "Joe, let's say you're going to ask me to go to the rec room after supper. When I say "No," you..."). While the issue is a hypothetical one, it is nevertheless realistic as it involves asking permission to attend an activity outside the home. After the youth successfully demonstrates the skill in the pretend situation, the staff member would return to the original issue for a final practice and successful resolution.

Feedback

Following the practice, the staff member provides enthusiastic praise, specific descriptions of the appropriate behavior, and awards positive consequences based on the demonstrated skills during practice.

Example: "Very good! You looked at me and said 'Okay.' That is the way to accept 'No.' You've earned 15 minutes of recreation time for practicing accepting 'No.'"

If further corrective feedback is needed, the staff member describes the inappropriate behavior and the necessary appropriate behaviors. The aggressive youth then has the opportunity to practice the entire skill or particular weak areas again. The total positive consequences awarded for the immediate practice session or sessions should not exceed one-half of the consequences that were lost. If multiple practice sessions are used during the teaching, staff member will need to adjust the privilege awards for practice accordingly to be sure that the total positive consequences earned for practice fall within the "up to one-half back" range.

Descriptive feedback and positive consequences serve to reinforce the appropriate behavior and improve the likelihood that the aggressive youth will engage in the appropriate behavior in the future. This type of feedback also demonstrates concern and support for the progress the youth is making. As a supportive mechanism, it also contributes to the positive relationship that is being developed between the youth and the child-care staff.

General Praise

The child-care staff remains supportive and positive throughout the interaction by praising the aggressive youth for a wide variety of appropriate behaviors. In particular, brief descriptive praise is provided for behaviors which indicate that the youth is paying attention and cooperating, such as looking at the staff, answering questions, and listening. Child-care staff pay close attention to those positive behaviors that have been difficult for that particular aggressive youth to display in the past (e.g. listening without interrupting, accepting criticism). If a youth has had difficulty accepting consequences in the past, the child-care staff always take the opportunity to reinforce the acceptance of a consequence whenever the youth is able to do so appropriately. The child-care staff should almost always provide a praise statement at the conclusion of the teaching to express support and to end the teaching on a positive note. This helps to reduce youth's anxiety about future teaching because they will remember that pre-vious teaching always ended on a positive basis.

Example: "You're doing a super job of accepting this consequence" or "Remember in the future to follow instructions just like we practiced. Good job!"

Praise throughout the interaction reinforces appropriate ongoing behavior, increasing the probability that such behaviors will occur in the future. Such praise also bolsters the positive relationships between the aggressive youth and child-care staff, and keeps teaching on a positive, success-oriented track.

In summary, the nine components of the Teaching Interaction can help aggressive youth learn appropriate alternative behaviors over time. While specific skills need to be mastered to effectively use a Teaching Interaction, it is much more than a technical process. Effective Corrective Teaching can only occur when there is a genuine concern for the youth and when there is a thoughtful, individualized approach to teaching. The Teaching Interaction is like any good tool. It is only effective when used by someone who cares about his or her "craft," who has taken the time and effort to become skillful, and who knows how, when, where, and why it should be used.

See an example of a complete Teaching Interaction in Figure 2.

FIGURE 2
TEACHING INTERACTION

Initial Praise/Empathy	"Thanks for looking at me while we're talking." "I know how much you were looking forward to the concert."
Description/Demonstration of Inappropriate Behavior	"When I said 'No,' you looked away and began to mumble."
Consequences	"For not accepting 'No,' you've lost your rec room privileges for the next 30 minutes."
Positive Correction	"You'll have the opportunity to earn back some of that consequence by practicing how to accept 'No.'"
Description/Demonstration of Appropriate Behavior	"Whenever someone has to tell you 'No,' whether it's a teacher, your parents, or me, here's what you need to do. You should look at the person, and acknowledge that you heard them by saying something like, 'Sure, I understand.' If you don't understand, calmly ask for a reason. And finally, do not argue or get angry about the decision."
Rationale	"You'll be more likely to be able to go on more activities because people will see you as more responsible."
Requests for Acknowledgment	"Do you understand?"
Practice	"Okay, Bill, now we're going to practice how to accept 'No.' I want you to ask me again if you can go to the concert. I am still going to say 'No,' but this time you need to look at me and say 'Okay' without mumbling."
Feedback	"Great! You looked at me and said 'Okay.' That is the way to accept 'No.' You've earned back 15 minutes of your rec room time."
General Praise	"Nice job! Keep trying, I know you'll do well."

Chapter Seven

Preventing Aggressive Behavior

To further enhance relationship development through teaching and help the aggressive youth improve problem behavior, child-care staff must take an active (versus reactive) approach to their role as treatment providers. Preventive or planned teaching procedures provide child-care staff with the tools to be active treatment providers. Therefore, preventive teaching should occur frequently to promote the development of new skills, to prevent problems from occurring, and to increase each youth's opportunities for success. Teaching preventively involves identifying skills an aggressive youth needs to learn, planning how to teach the skills, and conducting the teaching session. The types of skills most aggressive youth need to learn are listed in Appendix B.

The notion of "prevention" or Preventive Teaching is not only a part of the Boys Town Family Home Program, but also is a concept that is a part of society in general. One example of such teaching that is practiced routinely in our society is the fire drill. During fire drills, occupants of a building locate alarms and extinguishers and practice using exit routes. Such teaching reduces the chances of serious injury or death that might otherwise result should a real fire occur. Another example is taking a young child on a "safe

walk" to school at the beginning of the school year. Before school begins, the parent takes the youth on a walk to and from school. During this time, the parent can teach the youth the route, how to cross streets safely, and can point out block homes along the route where youth can go for assistance. Such teaching improves the youth's safety when he or she walks alone to school and reduces anxiety for both the youth and the parent. Taking the opportunity to review and teach about situations that will occur in the future can prevent problems.

Benefits of Preventive Teaching

In the Boys Town Model, Preventive Teaching provides many benefits to aggressive youth and child-care staff. Aggressive youth have experienced a great deal of criticism and received little praise for accomplishments from their parents (Farrington, 1978). In fact, parents of aggressive youth actually punish the prosocial behavior of their youth (Patterson, 1982). Preventive Teaching provides an excellent opportunity for child-care staff to reverse that process. Not only does Preventive Teaching improve the youth's chances of succeeding and reinforce prosocial behavior, but also provides child-care staff with more opportunities to teach. Those preventive opportunities are more likely to be successful and beneficial because they are occurring in the absence of problem behaviors. This means that anxiety levels and emotions are not at high levels for either the youth or the child-care staff. Instead, the learning process is facilitated by a comfortable, supportive, and relaxed environment.

Preventive Teaching occurs in the absence of problem behavior and is great for establishing relationships. Aggressive youth appreciate the inherent fairness, concern, and support involved in learning something new that will benefit them in the future (Willner et al., 1975). They also appreciate the opportunity to avoid engaging in inappropriate behaviors that will result in more difficulties for them. Their anxiety levels in the actual situations will be much reduced and they can more confidently approach new situations as well as recognize and remediate previous problems. In effect, Preventive Teaching allows child-care staff to break the "coercion" process by teaching aggressive youth appropriate ways of behaving.

Not only do the youth have the opportunity to comfortably succeed as a result of Preventive Teaching, but the success of child-care staff is enhanced as well. Indeed, the child-care staff's job satisfaction and personal satisfaction are improved as a result of their effective Preventive Teaching. This teaching helps avoid confrontations by positively and preventively establishing expectations and developing the youth's skills. Child-care staff can be more relaxed and comfortable with their youth in a wide variety of situations.

Preventive Teaching: What, When, Where, And How to Teach

The practical application of Preventive Teaching techniques involves knowing what to teach, when to teach, where to teach, and how to teach. In terms of content, Preventive Teaching sessions can focus on basic curriculum skills, advanced curriculum skills, or preparation for a specific set of circumstances. Basic curriculum skills are the focus of teaching for aggressive youth to quickly provide them with the prosocial skills they lack. As noted earlier, the basic curriculum skills for aggressive youth are provided in Appendix B. By using Preventive Teaching techniques to focus on these skills, the child-care staff members are helping the aggressive youth become open to and comfortable with the process of learning new skills. The process of learning new skills is frequently reinforcing. The teaching process itself becomes reinforcing. In effect, acquiring these basic skills makes the youth easier to teach. Having aggressive youth learn these basic skills thus facilitates teaching more advanced skills such as being honest, helping others, being sensitive to others, finding a job, etc.

In addition to focusing on basic and advanced curriculum skills that are frequently and typically called for, child-care staff members also preventively teach to specific or special circumstances. Usually, such circumstances are identified because child-care staff know each youth's strengths and weaknesses and anticipate situations that call for Preventive Teaching. For example, aggressive youth often have difficulty accepting criticism.

Knowing this, child-care staff need to focus a great deal of Preventive Teaching on the skill of "accepting criticism." Frequent Preventive Teaching sessions in the absence of the inappropriate behavior will increase the likelihood that the aggressive youth will be able to accept criticism when it is given. In summary, any skill can be taught by using Preventive Teaching procedures and many potentially difficult situations can be prepared for thorough Preventive Teaching.

Preventive Teaching can occur privately with individual youth or in small groups. Private work with an individual youth typically focuses on a youth's specific treatment goals or special situations that confront that youth. Small group sessions, or teaching that occurs with the family as a whole, typically focus on skill areas common to all youth. For example, rules pertaining to classroom behavior or home rules lend themselves to group teaching. Such group teaching allows the child-care staff to more efficiently teach necessary skills.

Preventive Teaching procedures make use of a number of Teaching Interaction procedures. The eight steps of Preventive Teaching are listed in Figure 1.

The steps of Preventive Teaching are:

Initial Praise

The child-care staff member establishes the tone of the interaction by beginning on a positive note. Aggressive youth will want to participate in Preventive Teaching more frequently and will be further motivated to learn when the opening statement is pleasant.

FIGURE 1
PREVENTIVE TEACHING PROCEDURES

1. Initial Praise
2. Explain the Skill and Give Examples
3. Describe or Demonstrate the Skill
4. Rationale
5. Request Acknowledgment
6. Practice
7. Feedback
    a. Praise
    b. Describe Behavior
    c. Positive Consequences
8. Future Practice/Praise

Example: "You really have done a fine job accepting criticism lately, Sam. When you receive criticism, you look at the person, you acknowledge the person, you don't argue, you correct the problem, and then you check back to let the person know you corrected the problem. That's great!"

Explain the Skill And Give Examples

The staff member conveys to the youth the nature of the discussion and identifies that specific skill area to be learned. The use of the skill in a variety of environments is described to help the youth generalize the use of the skill to a variety of antecedent conditions or settings.

Example: "I want to talk to you about another skill and that is 'making a request.' Making a request is important anytime you want something; for instance, if you want to watch television her in the home, if you're at school and need to get something out of your locker, or if you're at work and need to make a change in your schedule."

Describe or Demonstrate The Skill

The child-care staff member breaks the skill down into specific steps that the youth will be able to accomplish.

Example: "When you make a request, you need to look at the person you're speaking to, use a clear pleasant voice tone, and make your request in the form of a question. If your request is granted, remember to say 'Thank you.' If your request is denied, remember to accept 'No' for an answer.

The staff member may need to demonstrate the skill to clarify the verbal description as another assurance that the youth will understand. Demonstrations are especially helpful in communicating body posture, voice tone, facial expressions, and other behaviors that are difficult to describe verbally.

Example: "Let me show you what I mean. Let's pretend you are a school teacher and I'm you. I'll ask you if I can go to my locker and get a notebook. You tell me 'Okay, but be back in a couple of minutes.' Now, watch for those steps we just talked about."

Staff member (playing youth): "Ms. Smith, would it be all right if I go to my locker to get a notebook I need?"

Youth (playing teacher): "Yes, but be back in a couple of minutes."
Staff member (playing youth): "Thanks Ms. Smith. I'll be right back."

Rationale

The staff member should provide a rationale that describes how the new skill will benefit the youth.

Example: "If you make a request appropriately, it is more likely you will get to do what you want and you won't get in trouble for not asking."

Request for Acknowledgment

Throughout the interaction, the staff member should request acknowledgment from the youth to ensure his or her understanding and participation. This is particularly important after giving the youth a rationale to make sure the youth clearly understands the importance of the skill to his or her success.

Example: "Do you think you can remember those steps? Do you understand why asking permission is important?"

Practice

The youth should practice the skill he or she can become comfortable with it and so the staff member can determine the quality of his or her teaching.

Example: "Now I want you to try it. This time you ask me if you can listen to your stereo. After you request permission, I'll give you an answer. Okay? Let's practice!"

Youth: "Jane, would it be all right if I go to my room and listen to my stereo?"

Jane (staff member): "Yes, that would be fine if you listen to your stereo for 15 minutes."

Youth: "Great! I'll be back in 15 minutes."

Feedback

Praise

Describe Behavior

When practicing a new skill, a youth will likely do some things well and some things incorrectly. When providing feedback regarding the practice, the staff member should encourage the youth by descriptively praising those things done well, and specifically describing incorrect behaviors. The staff member should reteach that portion of the skill practiced incorrectly, and request the youth to practice again. It is important that the youth practice the skill until he or she has done all the steps correctly. After each practice, feedback should begin with descriptive praise and should be conveyed in a positive manner – calm and encouraging voice tone and posture. The staff member should describe, very enthusiastically, what the youth did correctly. If the youth is having consistent trouble practicing the skill, the staff member should check to see that the steps are not too difficult, that they were described specifically, and that the skill is age-appropriate. After the practice, the staff member should compliment the youth on his or her effort and arrange to practice more later. The practice should not be too lengthy as it can become punishing for both the youth and the staff member.

Example: "Nice job! You looked at me, made your request in the form of a question, waited for me to answer your question, and then you said you would be back in 15 minutes. There's only one thing you left out, which is really important; let the person know you appreciate getting to do what you want. You need to say 'Thank you' to the person. Let's try it again and this time remember to say 'Thank you.' Do you understand?" (Practice again and give feedback.)

Positive Consequence

The staff member provides a positive consequence to the youth for practicing the skill. Positive consequences can be natural or applied (planned ahead of time).

Example: "You have really done a good job practicing and learning the new skill of asking permission. For practicing the skill of 'making a request,' you have earned 15 minutes of phone time."

Future Practice/Praise

The child-care staff member lets the youth know that they will be practicing the skill again. The next session will follow fairly soon -- within five to fifteen minutes. Practices become less frequent as the youth begins to demonstrate the skill more consistently. After each practice, the staff member can continue to provide descriptive praise, descriptions of appropriate behavior, and positive consequences.

The staff member also should end the interaction as it began, positively, by praising the youth's participation and identifying those behaviors evident through the interaction.

Example: "Thanks for taking time to practice with me. You looked at me during the entire session and you asked some really good questions to help you understand what I meant. It's important now that we practice the skill of 'making a request' again real soon. Let's do another practice in about 15 minutes, okay?"

Figure 2 gives an example of a Preventive Teaching interaction using all eight steps.

In summary, Preventive Teaching builds relationships, fosters skill development, and increases the likelihood that youth will not act aggressively in the future. This procedure can be used to teach youth basic and advanced curriculum skills and to prepare youth for specific situations or circumstances. Preventive Teaching can be done on an individual basis or with small groups, depending upon the circumstances. Preventive Teaching procedures include initial praise, an explanation of the skill with examples, descriptions of appropriate behavior, rationales, requests for acknowledgment, practice, feedback, praise, and additional practice sessions. Preventive Teaching is a real key to an aggressive youth's success and to a child-care staff's sense of accomplishment as treatment providers.

There are two additional points to remember about Preventive Teaching. First, negative consequences are never given during a practice session. If a youth becomes noncompliant, end the session and proceed with Corrective Teaching, showing the youth a clear separation between the two procedures. Second, it's very important to practice all Preventive Teaching sessions to perfection so that youth have the best opportunities to learn and be successful, and to maintain consistent tolerance levels for all child-care staff.

FIGURE 2
PREVENTIVE TEACHING STEPS

1. Initial Praise	"Mary, you've been doing an excellent job of accepting 'No' for an answer according to the way we have practiced. You always say 'Okay' in a pleasant tone of voice and you don't argue like you have in the past. That's fantastic. It makes you more pleasant to be around and people are more likely to look for opportunities to say 'Yes' when they can."
2. Skill Explanation	"There's another skill I want to talk with you about, one you have had problems with in the past. That is assertiveness, or letting someone know, in an appropriate way, that you disagree with them."
3. Description/ Demonstration of Skill	"If you want to disagree with someone, or request a time to discuss the matter, you need to look at the person you're speaking to; use a neutral calm voice; remain relaxed and breathe deeply; clearly state your opinion or disagreement; listen to the other person; acknowledge other viewpoints or opinions; and thank the person for listening, regardless of the outcome."
4. Rationale	"If you can be assertive and express your opinion in an appropriate way, other people will be more likely to listen to you, you will be able to get your point across easier, and you might get your way more often."
5. Request for Acknowledgment	"Do you think you can remember those steps?"
6. Practice	"Now, why don't you try it. This time I'll tell you that you're late for school, and you can practice being assertive by telling me that it's Saturday, okay? What are the steps again? Great! Let's practice."
7. Feedback 　**a. Praise** 　**b. Describe Behavior** 　**c. Positive Consequences**	"Great job! You looked at me the whole time and remained calm. You didn't raise your voice or make any negative facial expressions. You stated your disagreement very clearly and you even used an 'I' statement. That was super. There's only one thing you left out, which is really important and that's to say 'Thank you.' Let's try it again and this time don't forget to say 'Thank you.' Okay? (Repeat and give feedback.) Excellent! You've earned...."
8. Future Practice/ Praise	"Thanks again, Mary, for being so cooperative during this practice. I'm really impressed with how quickly you learned this new skill. We'll have more opportunities today to practice again. Thanks."

Chapter Eight

Crisis Intervention: The Short-Term Solution

Child-care staff make a tremendous investment in helping each aggressive youth be successful as he or she learns new ways of behaving. Aggressive youth are very responsive to the praise, teaching, and relationships that they develop with child-care staff. However, at times, despite the best teaching efforts of the child-care staff, an aggressive youth will revert back to his or her old behavior patterns and become unresponsive or unwilling to follow instructions.

During this "out-of-control" time, typical teaching procedures and loss of privileges will not be effective. These behaviors will usually follow a time when child-care staff members have just requested the aggressive youth to follow an instruction, given some personal criticism, or said "No" to a request made by the youth. When an aggressive youth becomes a danger to self or others, has gone from anger to rage, or is behaving in a way that is seriously damaging to relationships, the primary goal of the child-care staff member is to help the youth calm down and once more be attentive to the teaching procedures that can help the youth solve the problem.

These "crisis intervention" procedures involve the teaching procedures that already have been described (see "Relationship Development and Effective Praise," "Teaching Alternatives to Aggressive Behavior," and "Preventing Aggressive Behavior" chapters) but the procedures are used in different ways and at different points in time to achieve the desired outcome: de-escalation of the youth's behavior. When the youth's behavior necessitates crisis intervention procedures, child-care staff should adhere to the appropriate organizational guidelines. (School counselors contact their school principal.) In the Boys Town Family Home Program, consultants or supervisors are to be notified immediately when crisis intervention procedures are employed.

While the crisis intervention procedures presented in this chapter have been extremely effective in mitigating out-of-control behaviors, the most desirable goal is to avoid and prevent the occurrence of such behaviors or incidents. One important step to help minimize episodes is to provide the aggressive youth with alternative ways of behaving through Preventive Teaching and continuous reinforcement of the desired behavior. This chapter will briefly review preventive procedures and then describe in detail the three general phases of the process used in the Boys Town Family Home Program to de-escalate crisis situations: Intensive Teaching.

General Preventive Procedures

The key to dealing with out-of-control behavior is prevention. Prevention begins the first day child-care staff begin working with aggressive youth. As the child-care staff use the skills and procedures that are taught in the training section that accompanies this manual, they will be able to prevent crisis situations from occurring. Effective Praise, Preventive Teaching, Teaching Interactions, and relationship building all contribute to youth success and a positive living environment.

Frequent Effective Praise (see "Relationship Development" and "Effective Praise" chapters) prevents aggressive outbursts by youth since appropriate behaviors are strengthened along with relationships. If youth are more frequently engaging in appropriate behaviors, they are less likely to engage in inappropriate behaviors.

Preventive Teaching (see "Preventing Aggressive Behavior" chapter) is one of the most critical procedures for maximizing youth success and minimizing crisis situations. Through this procedure, the child-care staff can set expectations, supportively teach, and strengthen the appropriate alternative behaviors, all in the absence of inappropriate behavior. The specific skills that need to be taught to prevent out-of-control behavior are "following instructions," "accepting criticism," and "accepting 'No' answers."

Teaching Interactions also help to prevent crisis situations because they allow the child-care staff to clearly set limits for youth behavior, teach alternative behavior, and allow for early intervention to head off potential problems. By intervening early when inappropriate behavior begins, child-care staff members will increase the probability that youth will respond to these typical preventive procedures.

Relationship-building (see "Relationship Development" and "Effective Praise" chapter) is another key to preventing aggressive outbursts by youth. Child-care staff members develop relationships as they praise and teach youth, spend time with them, advocate for them, pray with them, and demonstrate their love and concern through their teaching. In the process, the youth builds a special bond with the child-care staff. As this relationship grows, aggressive youth are less likely to engage in behavior that might disappoint the child-care staff and will be more likely to engage in the behaviors that will make the child-care staff proud of them.

Intensive Teaching Procedures

Despite the efforts of the most experienced and conscientious child-care staff, there will be times when an aggressive youth will not respond to the typical teaching procedures described previously in this sourcebook. This unresponsiveness may involve a wide range of behaviors. The aggressive youth may be passive, withdrawn, and silent. Or, the youth may be actively noncompliant as evidenced by arguing, swearing, or complaining. These problem behaviors may escalate to the point that the youth is making threats or damaging property.

Despite this variety of problem behaviors, there is a common element that indicates the need to use the Intensive Teaching procedures: The youth is engaging in ongoing behaviors and will not follow instructions to stop these behaviors. Ongoing behavior refers to any inattentive or problematic behavior that occurs prior to or during teaching that interferes with the original teaching agenda. In other words, a youth can be said to be "out of instructional control." Regardless of the severity or intensity of the situation, the same procedures can be used to help child-care staff regain instructional control so the youth can once again be taught.

To help conceptualize the process, the Intensive Teaching procedures have been grouped into three phases. However, it is important to note that the transition between stages is not always clear cut.

The three phases are the **preventive phase**, the **crisis intervention phase,** and the **teaching phase**. The **preventive phase** involves using the previously described teaching procedures to prevent problem behaviors from escalating, and to maintain control. If the preventive phase is ineffective, the child-care staff enters the **crisis intervention phase**. The goal of the crisis intervention phase is to calm the aggressive youth and help the youth regain control of his or her own behavior. After the child-care staff regains instructional control and the youth is once again responsible and attentive, the **teaching phase** occurs. During the **teaching phase**, the child-care staff continues to strengthen the aggressive youth's instruction-following skills. The child-care staff does Preventive Teaching with the youth on accepting consequences for his or her behavior and follow-up teaching on skills that would prevent future aggressive outbursts by the youth. Each of these "phases" are more thoroughly reviewed in the following pages.

Preventive Phase

The goal of the preventive phase is to prevent, if possible, short-term, intense behavior problems. The stops of the preventive phase are listed in Figure 1. These procedures focus on the child-care staff maintaining instructional control by preventing the aggressive youth's problem behaviors from escalating. In fact, most crisis situations are predictable, and therefore, preventable. Crisis situations are preventable, in part, because the antecedent conditions that often result in the loss of instructional control are fairly predictable. Frequently these conditions occur when a child-care staff is correcting a youth. Subsequently, the youth has difficulty accepting this criticism and then doesn't follow instructions. Other common antecedents to crisis situations with aggressive youth are receiving "No" answers or requests to follow an instruction, although the antecedent can differ from youth to youth. Child-care staff can learn the aggressive youth's idiosyncratic antecedents to crisis situations by using the observing and describing skills in the "Setting Boundaries" section of this sourcebook.

Since these antecedent conditions are predictable and observable, more serious behavior problems are frequently preventable. Often, instructional control can be regained without the behavior escalating. It is during this time that the staff's behavior becomes critical. Their behavior can cause the youth's aggression to escalate or it can defuse the situation and control can be regained quickly. Frequently, the difference between defusing a situation and creating a crisis is using empathy and giving the youth an opportunity to recover, rather than making them feel like they are being backed into a corner.

However, on occasion a youth will have experienced a difficult situation (e.g. a problem with relatives) that is unknown to the child-care staff. These problems can cause anger and frustration, and a single interaction with the child-care staff results in the loss of instructional control. In these cases, the preventive phase will be very brief, and the staff will go directly to the crisis intervention phase.

Since most aggressive outbursts by youth can be predicted and prevented, it is important to review the procedures that are used during the preventive phase to avoid the crisis. A general key is early intervention. At the first sign that an aggressive youth's ongoing behaviors are becoming inappropriate (e.g. harsh voice tone, not looking at staff, tight muscles), the child-care staff needs to intervene. A summary of the steps in the preventive phase are listed in Figure 1.

Empathy is frequently used as the child-care staff teaches or prompts (e.g. "I know that you're really upset but...."). Empathy statements can be effective tools in preventing out-of-control behavior. Child-care staff members should keep in mind that this is a very difficult time for the youth. They can afford to ease up and be more empathic in these intense situations and focus more on helping the youth regain emotional control. A series of empathy statements coupled with specific instructions are frequently more effective (e.g. "I know it is hard to listen to criticism, but you need to sit down so we can talk about it.") Reality statements also can be used in between instructions (e.g. "We're not getting anything accomplished this way.")

Child-care staff members also must be generous with the use of praise and empathy when the aggressive youth begins to comply

FIGURE 1
PREVENTIVE PHASE

STAFF BEHAVIOR	YOUTH BEHAVIOR
Original Teaching Issue	Neutral
Negative Consequence for Initial Behavior	First Inappropriate Behavior
Simple, Firm Instruction/Pause	Ongoing Behavior
Empathy	Ongoing Behavior
Simple, Firm Instruction/Pause	Ongoing Behavior
Additional Negative Consequence	Ongoing Behavior
Empathy	Ongoing Behavior
Simple, Firm Instruction/Pause	Ongoing Behavior
Cue Other Youth	Ongoing Behavior
Additional Negative Consequence	Ongoing Behavior
Empathy	Ongoing Behavior
Statement of Seriousness	Ongoing Behavior
Large Final Negative Consequence	Ongoing Behavior

with an instruction, (e.g. "It's not easy to calm down but you're showing a lot of maturity by sitting down.") The amount of time spent in providing empathy, instructions, etc., will vary from youth to youth depending on the aggressive youth's behavior. For a youth who is passively noncompliant, the child-care staff may make more use of these procedures. At any point that the aggressive youth begins to follow instructions and regains important attentive behaviors, an aggressive outburst has been prevented. Once the youth is attentive, regular teaching can resume.

At some point, the child-care staff may determine that empathy, instructions, and reality statements are not helping the aggressive youth. At this time, the child-care staff will systematically deliver a series of negative consequences. On the other hand, if an aggressive youth's inappropriate behavior escalates rapidly, the child-care staff may deliver a consequence after only one or two attempts at empathy or instructions.

A maximum of four negative consequences are given during the preventive phase. The first two consequences indicate the seriousness of the situation and help motivate the aggressive youth to engage in more appropriate behavior. Each of these three consequences are followed by more teaching, empathy, instructions, and praise for any appropriate behavior. While specific consequences are not rewarded for appropriate behavior, the child-care staff should indicate to the youth that he or she is beginning to earn back some positive consequences for appropriate behavior.

If the aggressive youth does not respond after the third negative consequence, **no additional small negative consequences** are given. This is because any further small consequences may only serve to escalate the behavior. As the aggressive youth continues to be unresponsive, the child-care staff will state the seriousness of the situation and give instructions in a firm voice tone (e.g. "This is getting really serious, we have to sit down and talk.") This statement of seriousness serves as a preventive instruction and is a cue to the youth that any further inappropriate behavior will result in a much larger consequence (e.g. "You are grounded for the weekend.") To maximize the effectiveness of the statement of seriousness in de-escalating the youth's behavior, child-care staff should standardize the statement. This will make the statement a clear antecedent to the aggressive youth that a large consequence will be administered quickly if his or her behavior does not change.

If the firm instruction and statement regarding the seriousness of the situation are not effective, the child-care staff delivers the final and largest of the negative consequences. This consequence is important regardless of whether it will have an impact on the aggressive youth's behavior. This signifies to the youth the response cost for a particular behavior, and also shows that guidelines are being established between the child-care staff and the aggressive youth. Because this response cost is involved in earning positive consequences or privileges again, the youth is motivated to learn skills that will help prevent out-of-control episodes, and will be less likely to present such problems in the future.

Figure 2 gives an example of a preventive phase dialogue when an aggressive youth's behavior continues to escalate.

FIGURE 2
PREVENTIVE PHASE DIALOGUE

1. Negative Consequence for Initial Behavior

CCS: "Okay. What I'd like to talk to you about is your request for an advance on your allowance. It's not possible at this time because you have received an advance on your allowance two of the last three weeks. I appreciate the way you made the request and the reasons you have, but this time I'll have to say 'No.'"

Bill: "Aw, I really need that money. I was planning on buying a new album."

CCS: "Bill, you did a good job of accepting 'No' by not swearing. However, now you're whining. For whining when I gave you that 'No' answer, you've earned an extra 30-minute chore."

Bill: "You are so unfair, I can't believe it."

Note: Bill begins to walk around the room.

2. Simple Firm Instruction

CCS: "Bill, you need to stop arguing so we can sit down and talk about your concerns."

3. Empathy

CCS: "Bill, I know it is hard to get a 'No' answer when you really want something."

Bill: "You don't know anything about how I feel."

4. Simple, Firm Instruction

CCS: "Bill, we are not getting anything accomplished this way. You need to stop talking and come over here and sit down."

Bill: "There's no way I'm coming over there."

FIGURE 2 (continued)
PREVENTIVE PHASE DIALOGUE

5. Additional Negative Consequence

CCS: "Bill, for not following instructions you have lost 30 minutes of phone time."

6. Empathy

CCS: "Bill, I know it must be hard for you to follow instructions right now but it is the only way we are going to get this problem solved."

Bill: "I am not going to follow instructions and you can't make me."

7. Cue Other Youth

CCS: "Guys, I am asking you to leave the room so Bill and I can work this problem out."

8. Additional Negative Consequence

CCS: "Bill, you've lost all privileges for the rest of the evening for not following instructions. If you stop arguing and come over and sit down, we can talk about the consequences."

9. Empathy

CCS: "I realize you're upset, but we can work this out."

Bill: "I can't believe how unfairly you treat me."

Note: Bill is now yelling and is still walking around.

10. Statement of Seriousness

CCS: "Bill, this is getting serious. You need to stop talking and sit down."

Bill: "I'm not going to stop talking. I know my rights."

11. Large Final Negative Consequence

CCS: "Bill, for not following instructions you are grounded for Saturday night."

Crisis Intervention Phase

The objective of the crisis intervention phase is to defuse the aggressive youth's behavior and regain instructional control. During this phase, no additional consequences are given (Figure 3). If the youth were to engage in some very serious behaviors (e.g. destruction of property), additional negative consequences would be added at a later time.

It is important to stay calm, talk in a non-threatening tone of voice, and talk slowly. Emotional control by child-care staff is the single most important factor. Do not yell or argue.

The child-care staff's behavior during the crisis intervention stage is similar to that of the preventive stage. There is a liberal use of empathy along with simple, firm instructions. The child-care staff will continue to point out the aggressive youth's ongoing inappropriate behavior and describe the alternative behavior to help guide the youth back to the point of following instructions (e.g. "You're walking around. Please sit down so we can begin to talk this out."). These instructions focus on the more overt, gross behaviors such as walking around, yelling, etc.

During this phase, the child-care staff continues to offer praise for approximations to instruction-following and other behaviors as they de-escalate and the youth begins to calm down ("Great, you've stopped yelling. I know that it is hard to stay calm when you're upset.").

As the crisis intervention continues, the aggressive youth's behavior may de-escalate and escalate several times. The goal is to have greater periods of improved behavior and increased compliance over a period of time. In addition to offering empathy, giving instructions, and praising approximations to appropriate behavior, the following guidelines will help the child-care staff resolve the crisis quicker.

FIGURE 3
CRISIS INTERVENTION PHASE

STAFF BEHAVIOR	YOUTH BEHAVIOR
Describe Appropriate Behavior	Ongoing Behavior
Describe Inappropriate Behavior	Ongoing Behavior
Simple, Firm Instruction/Pause	Ongoing Behavior
Empathy	Ongoing Behavior
Repeat Instruction/Pause	Ongoing Behavior
Positive Correction	Ongoing Behavior
Keep repeating these steps until the youth is under instructional control.	Follows All Instructions

Frequently during the crisis, the youth will bring up the loss of privileges resulting from the negative consequence earned for his or her inappropriate behavior. This is a time for the child-care staff member to respond with a form of positive correction, signaling to the youth the opportunity to earn back a portion of these privileges (e.g. "Yes I know that you have lost a lot of privileges, but you will have the opportunity to earn some back.").

It also is important for the child-care staff to remain calm and use an even, firm voice tone. Additionally, it is important to not respond to every comment the aggressive youth makes with an empathy or praise statement. Otherwise, this can be interpreted by the youth as "badgering" and may further escalate the aggressive outburst.

During the crisis intervention phase the aggressive youth may make demands (e.g. "I want to call my probation officer" or "You're not fair to me."). **It is very important for the child-care staff to not be drawn into content**. The best way to handle these demands, accusations, arguing behavior, etc., is to continue to offer empathy and indicate a willingness to discuss the issue as soon as the youth has calmed down (e.g. "You can sure make that phone call as soon as you come over and sit down, but right now you need to stop...."). By staying on task, the child-care staff can avoid the side issues that will only prolong the aggressive youth's out-of-control behavior and make it difficult for the child-care staff to de-escalate the youth's behavior.

As the child-care staff members work through the crisis with an aggressive youth, it is important for them to maintain physical proximity to the youth. The child-care staff needs to be careful not to invade the youth's private space, which could cause a physical confrontation. If the youth leaves the area, the child-care staff need to follow the youth, although not too closely.

If the aggressive youth decides to leave the main building, the child-care staff should not attempt to physically stop the youth by grabbing him or her or blocking an exit (dependent upon the age of the youth). If the youth begins to endanger self or others, the child-care staff will need to decide whether to restrain the youth or call for assistance. Any time restraint is used, the child-care staff should notify their immediate supervisor based on existing organizational guidelines.

The use of reality statements, coupled with the child-care staff's persistence and continued concern are also very helpful (e.g. "We're not accomplishing anything this way" or "I'm so concerned about you that I'll stay with you until we are able to work out this problem."). Statements of persistence and concern let the youth know that the child-care staff is not going to give up and will be there to help the youth no matter how long it takes.

The child-care staff member also will need to vary the intensity of his or her own behavior dependent upon the type of noncompliant behavior the aggressive youth is presenting. For example, if the youth is sullen, withdrawn, or passively defiant, the child-care staff will want to use more statements of empathy and more frequent instructions. If the child-care staff takes a passive role with passive-aggressive youth, the crisis situation will last that much longer. On the other hand, if the aggressive youth is highly agitated and verbally aggressive, the child-care staff will substitute periods of silence between empathy and instructions. This allows the youth to "run down" and avoids escalation that is caused by too frequent intervention by child-care staff.

Figure 4 gives an example dialogue of a crisis intervention exchange. The scenario used to illustrate the preventive phase is continued in the crisis intervention phase.

Teaching Phase

This phase begins when the youth is able to follow an instruction that was given and no subtle inappropriate behavior is occurring. The child-care staff continues to use empathy, praise, and positive correction to maintain instructional control. The child-care staff reiterates to the aggressive youth that he or she

FIGURE 4
CRISIS INTERVENTION DIALOGUE

Description of Appropriate Behavior	CCS: "Great, Bill. You've stopped walking around."
	Bill: "Yeah, now I suppose you want me to do something else."
Description of Inappropriate Behavior	CCS: "You're still yelling, Bill."
Simple, Firm Instruction/Pause	CCS: "You need to lower your voice tone, Bill."
Empathy	CCS: "I know this is tough, Bill. I know you're upset."
Repeat Instruction/Pause	CCS: "You need to lower your voice tone some more, Bill."
Positive Correction	CCS: "Bill, you have stopped walking around and you have lowered your voice tone. You are beginning to earn back privileges."

has earned back some privileges, but the amount of privileges earned back is not specified to the youth until the child-care staff has reiterated what privileges were lost. Prior to beginning a series of Corrective Teaching procedures, the child-care staff continues to test instructional control by giving a series of relevant instructions and praising compliance (e.g. "Why don't you move over a little closer to me? Thanks for following that instruction."). The steps of the teaching phase are listed in Figure 5.

Once the child-care staff is comfortable that the aggressive youth is able to maintain instructional control, some important Corrective Teaching must occur. However, the first task to review with the youth is the negative and positive consequences he or she earned. Praise for appropriate ongoing behavior (e.g. "You are really doing a good job of looking at me.") is very critical at this point.

After the consequences have been reviewed, the child-care staff begins to teach the skills of "following instructions," "appro-

FIGURE 5
INTENSIVE TEACHING PHASE

STAFF BEHAVIOR	YOUTH BEHAVIOR
Praise	Follows All Instructions
Review Negative Consequences:	Follows All Instructions
Loss of 30 minutes of phone time	Follows All Instructions
Loss of privileges for the remainder of the evening	Follows All Instructions
Grounding for Saturday evening	Follows All Instructions
Loss of car privileges for one week	Follows All Instructions
Review Positive Consequence:*	Follows All Instructions
Following Instructions	Follows All Instructions
Accepting Negative Consequences	Follows All Instructions
Practice Curriculum Skills:	Follows All Instructions
Following Instructions	Follows All Instructions
Appropriately Disagreeing	Follows All Instructions
Original teaching issue (e.g. Accepting "No")	Follows All Instructions
Apologizing	Follows All Instructions
Review Positive Consequences for	
curriculum skills practice*	Follows All Instructions
Teaching Interaction on the original teaching issue*	Follows All Instructions

*Not to exceed one-half of the total negative consequences earned in the Preventive Phase.

priately disagreeing," "accepting 'No'" (or whatever the original issue was) and "apologizing." Opportunities with positive consequences for appropriate behavior should occur. As mentioned in the "Teaching Alternatives to Aggressive Behavior" section, a youth can earn back up to half the negative consequences lost during the crisis situation. Positive consequences administered during practice opportunities must take into account the positive consequences just reviewed.

General Issues Relating To Intensive Teaching

The following issues and guidelines will help child-care staff in preventing and managing crisis situations. Another important issue regarding crisis situations is their evaluation. A method to help child-care staff evaluate and change crisis situation strategies is to chart the frequency, duration, and intensity of each crisis situation. This is of particular importance for aggressive youth because they will usually present persistent problems with regards to crisis situations. It is very difficult to detect improvements when the youth's behaviors are very serious or very frequent. Often these improvements are so slight that a particular strategy might be abandoned when, in fact, it may be working. Such charts can be shared with the youth so that progress can be reinforced and discussed. Child-care staff also can track the antecedents that frequently cause crisis situations for an aggressive youth so appropriate teaching can be done.

Child-care staff also willwant to minimize the attention or reinforcement that is available from other youth. The best way to avoid an audience is to establish a rule which basically states that upon the cue from a child-care staff member, all other youth are to leave the area and will be rewarded positive consequences for this behavior. The rule also should be specific and indicate where the youth should go and what activities may be engaged in (e.g. all youth can go to the recreation room).

In summary, it is best to avoid and minimize crisis situation episodes through teaching and by using the treatment program each day. However, when such episodes do occur, the child-care staff can successfully guide the aggressive youth back to a point that allows the typical teaching to be effective (Figure 6). Consistently using empathy, concern, and making it easy for a youth to recover will go a long way toward helping the aggressive youth better deal with their own emotions and problems.

There are some youth with whom these procedures as described may not work; these youth are the coercive youth (Patterson, 1982). With coercive youth, the progression of consequences used in the preventive phase will only make the situation worse. Each time a consequence is given, the coercive youth will escalate his or her behaviors in an apparent attempt to gain reinforcement for the out-of-control behavior. The consequences are not acting as response costs in this circumstance; instead, they are acting as stimuli for escalating behavior. The Intensive Teaching technique to use with coercive youth is to drop the preventive phase and go immediately to the crisis intervention phase, using a lot of empathy and encouragement statements. Consequences are not mentioned until the youth is calmed and in the final teaching phase.

It is important to note that child-care staff should not adopt this alternative technique merely because they think a youth is coercive. Child-care staff should first use the Intensive Teaching procedure with an out-of-control youth over a short period of time (e.g. seven to ten days) and observe what happens. If the youth drastically escalates his or her behaviors as a result of the consequences, then the alternative technique can be adopted for subsequent crisis interventions.

Figure 7 (next page) shows how the alternative technique might go.

FIGURE 6
RULES OF CRISIS INTERVENTION

1. Remain calm, do not accelerate your behavior when the aggressive youth does.

2. Keep repeating what the youth is doing (describe inappropriate) and what you want him or her to do (describe appropriate).

3. Make frequent empathy statements to let the youth know you're working with him or her.

4. Get on the same level – not too close and with an open posture.

5. Do not respond to content issues.

6. If the ongoing behavior continues, give one final negative consequence.

7. Tell the youth how positive points can be earned back (describe appropriate behavior).

8. Praise the youth for approximations to appropriate behavior.

9. When the aggressive youth has calmed down, talk about what happened and why it's a problem. Give consequences, explain how points can be earned back, and practice skills.

10. End the interaction on a positive note of continued support.

FIGURE 7
COERCIVE YOUTH ALTERNATIVE TECHNIQUE DIALOGUE

1. Negative Consequence for Initial Behavior

CCS: "Okay. What I'd like to talk to you about is your request for an advance on your allowance. It's not possible at this time because you have received an advance on your allowance two out of the last three weeks. I appreciate the way you made the request and the reasons you gave, but this time I'll have to say 'No.'"

Bill: "Aw, I really need that money. I was planning on buying a new album."

CCS: "Bill, you did a good job of accepting 'No' by not swearing. However, right now you're whining. For whining when I gave you that 'No' answer, you have earned an extra 30 minute chore."

Bill: "You are so unfair, I can't believe it."

Note: Bill begins to walk around the room.

2. Simple, Firm Instruction

CCS: "Bill, you need to stop arguing so we can sit down and talk about your concerns."

3. Empathy

CCS: "Bill, I know it is hard to get a 'No' answer when you really want something."

Bill: "You don't know anything about how I feel."

4. Simple, Firm Instruction

CCS: "Bill, we are not getting anything accomplished this way. You need to stop talking and come over here and sit down."

5. Empathy

CCS: "Bill, I know it must be hard for you to follow instructions right now, but it is the only way we are going to get this problem solved."

Bill: "I'm not going to and you can't make me."

6. Cue Other Youth

CCS: "Guys, I'm asking you to leave the room so Bill and I can work this problem out."

FIGURE 7 (continued)
COERCIVE YOUTH ALTERNATIVE TECHNIQUE DIALOGUE

7. Empathy	CCS:	"Bill, I realize you're upset, but let's talk this out."
	Bill:	"I can't believe how unfairly you treat me."
	Note:	Bill is now yelling and is still walking around.
8. Statement of Seriousness	CCS:	"Bill, this is getting serious. You need to stop talking and sit down."
	Bill:	"I'm not going to stop talking. I know my rights."
9. Describe Appropriate	CCS:	"Great, Bill! You've stopped walking around."
10. Describe Inappropriate	CCS:	"You're still yelling, Bill."
11. Simple, Firm Instruction	CCS:	"You need to lower your voice tone, Bill."
12. Empathy	CCS:	"I know this is tough, Bill. I know you're upset, but we can work through this."

Note: Continue on with numbers 9 through 12 until the youth is calmed down, then go to the Teaching Phase.

Chapter Nine

Problem-Solving: The Long-Term Solution

The aggressive youth has learned a pattern of behavior that is self-destructive and self-defeating with respect to successful community living. This pattern of behavior is played out daily in every facet of the youth's life (e.g. home, school, and work) and results in numerous interpersonal confrontations. While child-care staff should actively intervene when confrontations occur and teach the youth alternative behavior patterns, the ultimate goal is to help the youth develop effective problem-solving skills to avoid confrontations. Research has shown that aggressive youth will usually interpret interpersonal encounters as hostile and are less sensitive to interpersonal conflict (Kazdin, 1985). Additionally, they generate fewer alternative solutions to interpersonal encounters than other youth and their solutions are almost always aggressive in nature. Therefore, aggressive youth must be taught a step-by-step approach to solving interpersonal problems. At the same time that child-care staff members are teaching effective problem-solving skills to aggressive youth, they also will be developing their own listening skills, which will benefit them in all of their teaching with youth.

Problem-Solving Counseling

Problem-solving and effective listening involve actively teaching an aggressive youth how to explore his or her feelings and develop more appropriate responses to these feelings. Problem-solving can help youth learn to think through an issue before making a decision and can provide child-care staff with the opportunity to guide the decision-making process.

Child-care staff members should not appear shocked by anything the aggressive youth might say. It is very important for child-care staff to accept all feelings and convey to the youth that it is okay for him or her to express these feelings to the child-care staff. This helps the youth feel comfortable expressing emotions, fears, and concerns about intimate or embarrassing events. This also helps the child-care staff to better understand the youth and to put his or her current behavior in the context of those feelings.

In the Boys Town Family Home Program, problem-solving counseling goes beyond the traditional exploration of feelings and seeks to work out new, more appropriate responses to feelings. While it is okay to feel a certain way, it is not okay to behave in any way we want. Society holds us accountable for what we do.

Goals of Problem-Solving

The child-care staff's goals during problem-solving counseling sessions are to help the aggressive youth arrive at a viable solution to his or her problem and to teach the youth problem-solving skills. Because such counseling sessions also promote and establish trust between the child-care staff and the youth, another important goal is to build relationships during such sessions through expressions of concern, affection, respect, and interest in the youth's problems. As an aggressive youth confides in a child-care staff member and sees that such confidence is respected and is met with concern and helpfulness, he or she will feel more and more comfortable problem-solving with the child-care staff.

Use of Problem-Solving

Problem-solving counseling is most appropriate when an aggressive youth needs to develop a plan to deal with a problem. The problem may be one that he or she is currently experiencing or one that the youth is anticipating. The problem may involve the youth's parents, siblings, teachers, friends, employer, girlfriend, or boyfriend. Such problems can range from how to talk with an employer who has unfairly dealt with the youth, how to resist peer pressure, or deciding whether or not to participate in an activity. The problem-solving process also can be used retrospectively to help a youth make a better decision in the future. For example, child-care staff may use problem-solving counseling to help the aggressive youth review the problem that resulted in a fight with a peer at school and arrive at a more acceptable solution to a similar future situation.

There also are a number of situations when such problem-solving counseling is not appropriate. These situations include times when the child-care staff is attempting to teach an aggressive youth a new skill or when dealing with inappropriate behaviors such as skill deficiencies, rule violations, or inattentive ongoing behavior. Such youth behaviors require the consistent, concerned use of Preventive Teaching and Corrective Teaching, respectively. (See "Preventing Aggressive Behavior," and "Teaching Alternatives to Aggressive Behavior" chapters.) At times, the child-care staff may be tempted to counsel when a youth is passive and withdrawn or when the child complains about unfairness. In such cases, it is important to stay on task, regain the youth's attention and cooperation, and complete the various teaching agendas. Later, when the youth is calm and his or her behavior is appropriate, the child-care staff may choose to initiate a problem-solving counseling session.

There are times when serious issues occur and child-care staff should not attempt to counsel with the youth, but should seek professional guidance in counseling. For example, child-care staff can help a youth work through a divorce or death in his or her family, but sometimes they need to recognize that divorce and death are so traumatic that professional counseling is needed. Another example is when the youth threatens to commit suicide. Suicide threats should always be taken seriously and a supervisor or therapist should be consulted immediately.

Counseling should not be attempted when the youth is under the influence of drugs or alcohol. Due to the youth's intoxication, he or she will not be capable of good decision-making, therefore, no counseling or consequences should be attempted until the youth is sober. In fact, counseling may provoke violent behavior on the part of the aggressive youth.

Child-Care Staff Counseling Behaviors

The following qualities are critical if child-care staff members are to achieve effective and successful problem-solving counseling with aggressive youth. Mastering these qualities requires practice and reflection on the part of child-care staff, and will enhance their effectiveness in working with aggressive youth.

1. **Listening Skills:** Child-care staff who have good listening skills encourage the youth to discuss issues and express feelings. The child-care staff member can indicate that he or she cares about what the youth is saying and respects the youth's input by looking at him or her, not interrupting, frequently nodding, and generally being attentive.

2. **Verbal Behavior:** The child-care staff can keep the aggressive youth on the subject and involved by offering verbal encouragement and praise (e.g. "It's really good that you're thinking this through."). Asking clarifying questions and requesting more information will encourage the youth to participate even more (e.g. "Tell me a little more about what happened after that.").

3. **Empathy:** Providing empathy during the discussion lets the youth know that the child-care staff is trying to understand the youth's feelings and point of view (e.g. "That must be very upsetting to you" or "It looks like you're really angry about that."). Empathy is very important in establishing rapport with an aggressive youth and encouraging him or her to discuss issues.

4. **Physical Proximity:** Child-care staff will want to avoid sitting behind a desk or table or having other physical barriers that could interfere with the youth feeling that the child-care staff is accessible. Sitting on a couch with a youth or sitting in a chair directly across from him or her establishes a relaxed and comfortable setting for the youth.

While all these qualities are important to facilitate problem-solving, they also are important to include in the child-care staff's day-to-day interactions with each aggressive youth. The child-care staff need to express care and concern, to listen, to offer empathy, etc., in other interactions with a youth as well as during problem-solving. There should not be a dramatic change in the child-care staff's behavior when problem-solving with youth. Rather, nurturing and caring behavior occurs daily. When child-care staff members consistently express their concern and act in ways that demonstrate their commitment, the aggressive youth are more likely to come to them with problems.

Problem-Solving Procedures

The child-care staff members guide the counseling and rational problem-solving process by using the **SODAS** method, a revision of a counseling process developed by Jan

Roosa (1973). **SODAS** is an acronym that stands for the following steps:

S Defining the problem **situation**.
O Examining **options** available to deal with the problem.
D Determining the **disadvantages** of each option.
A Determining the **advantages** of each option.
S Deciding on the **solution/simulation**.

While using the **SODAS** method the child-care staff will need to be sure to engage in all the supportive nonverbal and verbal behaviors previously discussed. Each of the **SODAS** components is reviewed in more detail on the following pages.

Situation

The problem-solving process begins with the child-care staff helping the aggressive youth clearly define the situation or problem. In some cases the youth initially will present vague and emotional descriptions (e.g. "I'm sick of school" or "My folks don't care what happens to me."). The child-care staff can use general clarifying questions or statements to help the aggressive youth more fully describe the issues (e.g. "Why don't you explain that some more."). However, it may be necessary for the child-care staff to ask direct, specific questions (e.g. "Why are you sick of school?" or "Did something happen during your home visit?"). By calmly and skillfully asking specific questions, the child-care staff can keep the youth involved and help the youth articulate a realistic description of the situation.

As the child-care staff member asks questions, he or she needs to provide empathy, concern, and encouragement as the youth responds. Without empathy, concern, and encouragement statements, the series of specific questions becomes more of an interrogation that is apt to cause the aggressive youth to withdraw.

As the youth more clearly defines the situation, the child-care staff needs to summarize what the youth is saying. This summarization is particularly important before any options are discussed. The summarization helps assure the child-care staff that all relevant information has been reviewed and that the child-care staff has accurately perceived the youth's situation. If the summarization is inaccurate or incomplete, the aggressive youth has the opportunity to correct any misperceptions. This is especially important at this point since the remainder of the process is built around the defined situation. Without an accurate or clearly defined situation, it will be difficult to generate useful options and a viable solution.

Options

After the situation is clearly defined, the child-care staff helps the youth generate options in the form of potential solutions to the problem. It is important to have the aggressive youth generate the alternatives that might solve the problem. The child-care staff member needs to remember that the goal is to have the youth develop the ability to solve problems as well as arrive at a solution.

To help the youth generate options, the child-care staff needs to specifically ask the youth how he or she might solve the problem or deal with the situation (e.g. "Can you think of a way to handle that?" or "What do you think you can do about this?"). After an option is suggested by the youth, the child-care staff needs to continue to solicit additional options (e.g. "Can you think of any other ideas?").

Initially, aggressive youth may have difficulty generating options. Also, the suggestions offered may not be very helpful or realistic. Whenever a youth does give an option, it is important for the child-care staff to remain nonjudgmental. The child-care staff can remain nonjudgmental by commenting positively about the youth's participation in the process (e.g. "Well good, you've come up with a second option. You're really trying to think this through."). The child-care staff can also offer a neutral comment and a prompt for more options (e.g. "Okay, that's one option. Can you think of another one?").

Remaining nonjudgmental can be difficult for the child-care staff, especially when the aggressive youth suggests an option that would only result in greater difficulty for the youth (e.g. "I'll just have to punch him out."). The child-care staff member needs to remember that his or her role at this point is just to get the youth to generate options. In that sense, this phase of the process is like "brainstorming." If a staff member becomes judgmental by discounting or denying the youth the opportunity to come up with options, the staff member will harm his or her relationship with the youth and diminish the likelihood that the youth will come to him or her with problems. Discretion by the child-care staff member is of the utmost importance as there may be times when the youth tests known limits and attempts to manipulate the staff member. Consistent tolerance levels by the staff member are crucial to eliminate such tactics by the youth. It is the next phase of examining the advantages and disadvantages that allows the child-care staff to help the youth judge the "wisdom" of the suggested options.

During the option phase, the child-care staff member may give his or her suggestions as well. However, this should be done only after the youngster has given all of his or her ideas. The child-care staff may want to phrase the option as a questions (e.g. "How about talking to the teacher after class?") so that the youth still feels involved in the process. Over time, aggressive youth will be better able to generate options and will be more comfortable doing so.

Disadvantages and Advantages

After a number of options have been generated, the child-care staff member helps the youth think through the disadvantages and advantages. Each option is examined in turn and the disadvantages and advantages are discussed. In a sense, the child-care staff member is trying to teach the aggressive youth that there is a cause-and-effect relationship between making decisions and what happens to him or her.

As in generating options, it is important to have the youth think through the advantages and disadvantages. Again, the child-care staff's role is to skillfully guide the youth by asking general questions (e.g. "Can you think of any problems if you do that?" or "Are there any benefits for doing that?"). If the youth has difficulty thinking through the disadvantages and advantages, the child-care staff can help by asking more specific questions (e.g. "Well, what do you think your teacher will do if you start a fight in his class?" or "Do you think she might be more willing to listen to you if you did that?").

There may be a number of disadvantages and advantages for any given option. Again, since a goal is to help the youth learn to think, it is also important in this phase to solicit additional disadvantages and advantages (e.g. "Can you think of any other advantages? Any other problems?"). During the process, it is still important for the child-care staff to remain nonjudgmental and not to argue with an aggressive youth about his or her perceptions of the disadvantages and advantages. This can be difficult when the youth seems enthusiastic about the advantages of an option that may not be realistic or could be problematic (e.g. "Yeah, it'd be great to fight it out because then he'd leave me alone and everybody would think I was bad."). Rather than argue about the advantage, the child-care staff can simply acknowledge the youth's view (e.g. "Okay, so you think that an advantage would be...."). Later, the child-care staff can guide the youth's judgment during the discussion of the disadvantages (e.g. "What happens if you don't win?", "Could you get hurt?", or "What will your boss do if he hears you've fought with another employee?").

If the aggressive youth clearly does not see or cannot be directed to verbalize an important advantage or disadvantage, the child-care staff should offer his or her viewpoint and allow the youth to react.

After the disadvantages and advantages for the options have been discussed, the child-care staff needs to summarize by reviewing each option and the associated advantages and disadvantages. This summary further helps the youth see the cause-and-effect relationships.

Solution/Simulation

This phase involves having the aggressive youth select the solution and preparing the youngster to successfully implement it by conducting any necessary "simulations" or role-play sessions. As a result of examining disadvantages and advantages, the youth typical selects a workable option. It may not always be the best option from the child-care staff's point of view, but it must be a realistic option. It is important that the youth feel some ownership of the choice because he or she is more likely to be committed to make the option work.

After the aggressive youth has selected an option, the child-care staff should encourage and reassure the youth that he or she can successfully implement the solution. In making the youth comfortable with the solution, the child-care staff can answer any questions the youth may have about how to successfully implement it. Another important aspect of improving the aggressive youth's chance of success is for the child-care staff to set up a role-play or practice session. These role-play sessions should be as realistic as possible. Often the child-care staff will know the people the youth will need to interact with as he or she implements the solutions (e.g. parents, friends, employers, teacher). Because the child-care staff knows these individual, he or she can behave in ways similar to those people. For example, if an employer is fairly abrupt and somewhat stern, the child-care staff can best help the youth by portraying the employer in that manner. The role-play can be made more realistic by presenting the youth with several possible responses so that he or she will be more comfortable and more likely to succeed.

The child-care staff needs to express confidence in the aggressive youth's ability to implement the solution. However, the child-care staff should not promise the youngster that the solution will work. As the practice session ends, the child-care staff should prompt the youth to check back after he or she has tried to implement the solution. If the youth succeeds in solving the problem, the child-care staff will want to praise the youth for doing so and for going through the problem-solving session. If the solution was not workable, the child-care staff needs to be supportive and empathic. The child-care staff and aggressive youth can then return to the **SODAS** format to find a more successful solution.

In summary, learning to problem-solve is a complex task, but it is critical to an aggressive youth's eventual success. Learning how to problem-solve is so important that it is reasonable to have a youth earn some type of reward to reinforce his or her cooperation. Further, because aggressive youth have "solved" their problems in inappropriate ways in the past (e.g. running away, becoming angry), it is important to praise a youth when her or she indicates a desire to talk about a problem (e.g. "I have a problem at work. Can you talk with me about it?").

The complete use of the **SODAS** format during a private counseling session will be important in teaching rational problem-solving skills to aggressive youth. However, there are many other types of formal and informal activities that facilitate modeling and directly teaching this problem-solving approach. Informally, there will be opportunities for discussions that may be prompted by television shows or world events. As an aggressive youth expresses his or her options and point of view, it provides the child-care staff with some ideal opportunities to help this youth to think, to weigh options, and discuss the possible results of his or her views and values. For example, the child-care staff member and the youth may be riding in a van together and observe a young person driving a car as it speeds through an intersection, runs a red light and squeals its tires. At that point, the aggressive youth may comment on how he or she can hardly wait until he or she can have a car and be "bad." The child-care staff member could use this opportunity to ask if the youth sees any problems (disadvantages) with running red lights or speeding. The child-care staff member also could ask the youth for ideas (options) about how to impress people with a car without engaging in unsafe or illegal activities. Such informal discussions can help aggressive youth learn to think ahead, to get his or her needs met in appropriate ways and to connect his or her actions with future possible consequences. All these behaviors are keys to thinking and problem-solving.

There will be more formal opportunities to use the **SODAS** method when an aggressive youth needs to develop a plan for the future. For instance, planning for a career, employment, college, or deciding how to develop an area of interest, all lend themselves to the **SODAS** process.

There may be times when the child-care staff will initiate a counseling session and use the **SODAS** process the help an aggressive youth develop a plan for more personal issues (e.g. making friends, personal hygiene, etc.).

It is important for child-care staff to take a future-oriented approach to such sessions as well as being receptive to sessions initiated by an aggressive youth.

Problem-solving counseling has two important goals – to help aggressive youth arrive at sound solutions to their problems and to teach them how to solve problems in a systematic, rational way. The **SODAS** process, coupled with important quality components (e.g. empathy, listening skills, etc.) can help child-care staff accomplish both goals.

Appendix A

SHORT CHORES

1. Scrub burner on stove
2. Clean kitchen or bathroom sink
3. Sweep floor
4. Clean toilet bowl
5. Clean mirror in bathroom
6. Empty dishwasher
7. Fold one load of laundry
8. Vacuum carpet in one room
9. Dust one room
10. Wipe down one wall
11. Sweep front or back sidewalk
12. Clean tub or shower
13. Clean out kitchen cabinet
14. Clean out refrigerator
15. Scrub floor
16. Polish furniture
17. Water plants
18. Wash car
19. Vacuum car
20. Clean out garbage can
21. Pick up litter in the yard
22. Clean up the dog "dirt" in the yard
23. Clean out ashtrays
24. Sweep out garage
25. Wipe down kitchen cabinets
26. Wash dishes
27. Clean out fireplace
28. Bring firewood in
29. Help with ironing

LONG CHORES

1. Wash windows
2. Clean mold off tiles in shower
3. Clean mold off windows
4. Scrub outside of pots and pans
5. Rake leaves
6. Pull weeds
7. Chop wood and/or stack it
8. Wash down the outside of the house
9. Clean the rain gutters
10. Mow the lawn and rake it
11. Edge the grass
12. Clean the oven

Source: Patterson, G.R., & Forgatch, M.S. (1987). **Parents and Adolescents: Part I. The Basics**. Eugene, OR: Castalia Publishing Company.

Appendix B
SOCIAL SKILLS CURRICULUM

ASKING FOR HELP

1. Look at the person.
2. Ask person if he or she has time to help you (now or later).
3. Clearly describe the problem or what kind of help you need.
4. Thank the person for helping you.

ACCEPTING CRITICISM OR A CONSEQUENCE

1. Look at the person.
2. Say "Okay."
3. Don't argue.

FOLLOWING INSTRUCTIONS

1. Look at the person.
2. Say "Okay."
3. Do what you've been asked right away.
4. Check back.

CORRECTING ANOTHER PERSON (OR GIVING CRITICISM)

1. Look at the person.
2. Remain calm and use a pleasant voice tone.
3. Begin with a positive statement, some praise, or by saying "I understand...."
4. Be specific about the behaviors you are criticizing.
5. Offer a rationale for why this is a problem.
6. Listen to the other person's explanation. Avoid any sarcasm, name-calling, or "put-down" statements.

ACCEPTING "NO" FOR AN ANSWER

1. Look at the person.
2. Say "Okay."
3. Stay calm.
4. If you disagree, ask later.

MAKING A REQUEST (ASKING A FAVOR)

1. Look at the person.
2. Use a clear, pleasant voice tone.
3. Make your request in the form of a question by saying "Would you..." and "Please...."
4. If your request is granted, remember to say "Thank you."
5. If your request is denied, remember to accept "No" for an answer.

PROBLEM-SOLVING A DISAGREEMENT

1. Look at the person.
2. Remain calm. Use a pleasant voice.
3. Identify options for solving the disagreement.
4. Evaluate the potential consequences.
5. Choose the best solution for the situation.
6. Be open to views of the other person.

REPORTING WHEREABOUTS

1. Look at person (if report is made in person).
2. Use a pleasant voice tone.
3. Explain where you'll be, when you'll be back.
4. Wait for acknowledgment.
5. Thank person for listening.
6. Let person know if plans change.

RESISTING PEER PRESSURE

1. Look at the person.
2. Use a calm, assertive voice tone.
3. State clearly that you do not want to engage in the inappropriate activity.
4. Suggest alternative activity. Give a reason.
5. If the person persists, continue to say "No."
6. Ask the peer to leave or remove yourself from the situation.

ASSERTIVENESS

1. Look at the person.
2. Use a neutral, calm voice.
3. Remain relaxed and breathe deeply.
4. Clearly state your opinion or disagreement. Avoid emotional terms.
5. Listen to the other person.
6. Acknowledge other viewpoints and opinions.
7. Thank the person for listening.

References

Ackerson, L. (1931). **Children's behavior problems** (Vol. 1). Chicago: University of Chicago Press.

Bedlington, M.M., Solnick, J.R., Braukmann, C.J., Kirigin, K.A., & Wolf, M.M. (1979, August). The correlation between some parenting behaviors, delinquency and youth satisfaction in Teaching-Family group homes. In J.R. Solnick (Chair), **Family interaction and deviant behavior.** Symposium conducted at the 87th Annual Convention of the American Psychological Association, New York.

Behar, D., & Stewart, M.A. (1982). Aggressive conduct disorder in children. **Acta Psychiatric Scandinavia, 65,** 210-220.

Braukmann, C.J., Kirigin, K.A., & Wolf, M.M. (1976). **Achievement place: The researcher's perspective.** Paper presented at the 84th Annual Convention of the American Psychological Association, Washington, DC.

Brown, G.L., Ebert, M.H., Goyer, P.F., Jimerson, D.C., Klein, W.J., Bunney, W.E., & Goodwin, F.K. (1982). Aggression, suicide and serotonin: Relationships to CSF amine metabolites. **American Journal of Psychiatry, 139,** 741-745.

Cadoret, R.J. (1978). Psychopathology in adopted-away offspring of biological parents with antisocial behavior. **Archives of General Psychiatry, 35,** 176-184.

Christiansen, K.O. (1974). Seriousness of criminality and concordance among Danish twins. In R. Hood (Ed.), **Crime, criminology and public policy** (pp. 63-67). London: Heinemann.

Cloninger, C.R., Reich, T., & Guze, S.B. (1978). Genetic-environmental interactions and antisocial behaviour. In R.D. Hare & D. Schalling (Eds.), **Psychopathic behaviour: Approaches to research** (pp. 225-237). Chichester: John Wiley & Sons.

Crow, R. (1974). An adoption study of antisocial personality. **Archives of General Psychiatry, 31,** 785-791.

Disjoin, T.J., Loeber, R., Stouthamer-Loeber, M., & Patterson, G.R. (1984). Skill deficits and male adolescent delinquency. **Journal of Abnormal Child Psychology, 12,** 37-54.

Edelbrock, C. (1983). **The antecedents of antisocial behavior: A cross-sectional analysis.** Unpublished manuscript, University of Pittsburgh School of Medicine.

Farrington, D.P. (1978). The family background of aggressive youths. In L.A. Hersov, M. Berger, & D. Schaffer (Eds.), **Aggressive and antisocial behavior in childhood and adolescence** (pp. 73-94). Oxford, England: Pergamon Press.

Forgatch, D.P. (1988, February). **A social learning approach to family therapy.** Paper presented at the Taboroff Child and Adolescent Psychiatry Conference on Conduct Disorders in Children and Adolescents, Snowbird, UT.

Freedman, B.J., Rosenthal, L., Donahue, L.P. Jr., Schlundt, D.G., & McFall, R.M. (1978). A social-behavioral analysis of skill deficits in delinquent and nondelinquent adolescent boys. **Journal of Consulting and Clinical Psychology, 46,** 1448-1462.

Gilbert, G.M. (1957). A survey of "referral problems" in metropolitan child guidance centers. **Journal of Clinical Psychology, 13,** 37-42.

Glueck, S., & Glueck, E.T. (1950). **Unravelling juvenile delinquency.** Cambridge, MA: Harvard University Press.

Glueck, S., & Glueck, E.T. (1968). **Delinquents and nondelinquents in perspective.** Cambridge, MA: Harvard University Press.

Hardy, R. (1988). **Behavior analysis: A computer-based tutorial** (computer program). DePere, WI: St. Norbert College.

Hetherington, E.M., & Martin, B. (1979). Family interaction. In H.C. Quay & J.S. Werry (Eds.), **Psychopathological disorders of childhood** (2nd ed.) (pp. 247-302). New York: John Wiley & Sons.

Hirschi, T. (1969). **Causes of delinquency.** Berkeley: University of California Press.

Hirschi, T. & Hindeland, M.J. (1977). Intelligence and delinquency: A revisionist's review. **American Sociological Review, 42,** 571-587.

Kanfer, F.H., & Saslow, S. (1969). Behavioral diagnosis. In C.M. Franks (Ed.), **Behavior therapy: Appraisal and status** (pp. 417-444). New York: McGraw-Hill.

Kazdin, A.E. (1985). **Treatment of antisocial behavior in children and adolescents.** Homewood, IL: The Dorsey Press.

Kazdin, A.E. (1987). Treatment of antisocial behavior in children: Current status and future directions. **Psychological Bulletin, 102,** 187-203.

Klein, N.C., Alexander, J.F., & Parsons, B.Y. (1977). Impact of family system interventions on recidivism and sibling delinquency: A model of primary prevention and program evaluation. **Journal of Consulting and Clinical Psychology, 45,** 469-474.

Ledingham, J.E., & Schwartzman, A.E. (1984). A 3-year follow-up of aggressive and withdrawn behavior in childhood: Preliminary findings. **Journal of Abnormal Child Psychology, 12,** 157-168.

Lesser, G.S. (1959). The relationships between various forms of aggression and popularity among lower-class children. **Journal of Educational Psychology, 50,** 20-25.

MacFarlane, J.W., Allen, L., & Honzik, M.P. (1954). **A developmental study of the behavior problems of normal children 21 months and 14 years.** Berkeley: University of California Press.

Maerov, S.L., Brummett, B, Patterson, G.R., & Reid, J.B. (1978). Coding of family interactions. In J.B. Reid (Ed.), **A social learning approach to family intervention** (pp. 21-37). Eugene, OR: Castalia.

Mattsson, A, Schalling, D., Olweus, D., Low, H., & Svensson, J. (1980). Plasma testosterone, aggressive behavior, and personality dimensions in young male delinquents. **Journal of the American Academy of Child Psychiatry, 19,** 476-490.

McCord, W., McCord, J., & Zola, J.K. (1959). **Origins of crime.** New York: Columbia University Press.

Mednick, S.A. (1978). You don't need a weatherman! In L. Otten (Ed.), **Colloquim on the correlates of crime and the determinants of criminal behavior** (pp. 133-151). Arlington, VA: MITRE.

Mednick, S.A., & Hutchings, B. (1978). Genetic and psychophysiological factors in asocial behaviour. In R.D. Hare & D. Schalling (Eds.), **Psychopathic behaviour: Approaches to research** (pp. 239-253). Chichester: John Wiley & Sons.

Nye, F.I. (1958). **Family relationships and delinquent behavior.** New York: John Wiley & Sons.

Patterson, G.R. (1982). **Coercive family process.** Eugene, OR: Castalia.

Patterson, G.R., DeBaryshe, B.D., & Ramsey, E. (1989). A developmental perspective on antisocial behavior. **American Psychologist,** February, 329-335.

Patterson, G.R., Dishion, T.J., & Bank, L. (1984). Family interaction: A process model of deviancy training. **Aggressive Behavior, 10,** 253-267.

Patterson, G.R., Dishion, T.J., & Reid, J.B. (1989). **A social learning approach: Volume 4, a coercion model.** Eugene, OR: Castalia.

Patterson, G.R., & Forgatch, M. (1987). **Part 1: The basis, parents and adolescents living together.** Eugene, OR: Castalia.

Patterson, G.R., & Stouthamer-Loeber, M. (1984). The correlation of family management practices and delinquency. **Child Development, 55,** 1299-1307.

Peter, V.J. (1986). **What makes Boys Town so special.** Boys Town, NE: Father Flanagan's Boys' Home.

Raz, E. (1977). **The relationship of youth ratings and future delinquent behavior.** Unpublished mater's thesis. Lawrence, KS: University of Kansas.

Robins, L.N. (1966). **Deviant children grown up**. Baltimore: Williams & Wilkins.

Robins, L.N. (1978). Sturdy childhood predictors of adult antisocial behavior: Replications from longitudinal studies. **Psychological Medicine, 8,** 611-622.

Roosa, J.B. (1973). **SOCS: Situations, options, consequences, simulation: A technique for teaching social interactions.** Unpublished paper presented to the American Psychological Association, Montreal.

Rutter, M., & Giller, H. (1983). **Juvenile delinquency: Trends and perspectives.** New York: Penguin Books.

Rutter, M., Tizard, J., & Whitmore, K. (Eds.) (1970). **Education, health and behavior.** London: Longmans.

Sheard, M.H. (1975). Lithium in the treatment of aggression. **Journal of Nervous and Mental Disease, 160,** 108-118.

Snyder, J. Dishion, T.J., & Patterson, G.R. (1986). Determinants and consequences of associating with deviant peers during preadolescence and adolescence. **Journal of Early Adolescence, 6,** 29-43.

Sturge, C. (1982). Reading retardation and antisocial behavior. **Journal of Child Psychology and Psychiatry, 23,** 21-31.

Wadsworth, M. (1979). **Roots of delinquency: Infancy, adolescence and crime.** New York: Barnes & Noble.

Werry, J.S., & Quay, H.C. (1971). The prevalence of behavior symptoms in younger elementary school children. **American Journal of Orthopsychiatry, 41,** 136-143.

West, D.J. (1982). **Delinquency: Its roots, careers and prospects.** Cambridge, MA: Harvard University Press.

Willner, A.G., Braukmann, C.J., Kirigin, K.A., Fixsen, D.L., Phillips, E.L., Wolf, M.M. (1975, September). Training and validation: Youth preferred social behavior with child care personnel. In C.J. Braukmann (chair), **New directions in behavioral group home research.** Symposium conducted at the 83rd Annual Convention of the American Psychological Association, Chicago.

Wolfgang, M.E., Figlio, R., & Sellin, T. (1972). **Delinquency in a birth cohort.** Chicago: University of Chicago Press.